I0458806

POSSIBILITY TO PROSPERITY

POWERFUL JOURNEYS OF TRANSFORMING PASSION INTO *Purpose*

by:

ANISA CRESPO & NATOSHA NAVARRO

along with:

14 INSPIRING AUTHORS

ISBN: 978-1-966798-93-4

Dedication

From Anisa & Natosha

To every soul who saw our vision before it was fully formed...
To those who invested in us—not just with money, but with belief, encouragement, time, and trust...

Thank you.

Your support wasn't just appreciated—it was foundational.
You didn't just help us grow a business.
You helped us build a movement, a mission, and a legacy that's now impacting thousands of women around the world.

Because of you, we dared to dream bigger, move faster, and rise higher than we ever imagined.
Your faith in us fueled our faith in ourselves.
And for that, we are forever grateful.

This book, this moment, and everything that's still to come...
It's dedicated to you.

With love,
Anisa & Natosha

TABLE OF CONTENTS

INTRODUCTION 7

Preface 9

From Scarcity Mindset to Six-Figure Months Through Passion, Purpose, and a Promise to Myself
By Anisa Crespo 11

Born for More, Built to Rise
By Natosha Navarro 28

From Shackled to Sovereign: How I Turned Inner Fire Into a Mission-Driven Life
By Jen Conkey 41

Never Again
By Stacy Conkey..53

I Am the Possibility: From Silence to Sovereignty
By Thyra Newby 66

I Was Poor Until I Learned to See
By Ariel Faith.. 78

Becoming HER: Possibility to Prosperity
By Tomeka Jones 90

From Scarci-Tea' to Prosperi-Tea' to Generosi-Tea!
By Anna Barboza Lugo.. 110

Prosper God's Way: A Journey to Freedom, Clarity, and Abundance
By Erica Elliott 123

Built from Chaos: My Son, My Spark, and the Unmasked Me
By Tazz De Souza...133

Walking by Faith, Living in Fullness
By Elizabeth Meigs..149

The Aligned Path: Turning What You Love into Lasting Profit
By Latraila Tolbert 165

The Mirror That Made Prosperity Inevitable
By Wendy Johnson.. 177

Finding Home: When Life's Detour Becomes the Path
By Dr. Araba Afenyi-Annan 199

From Sparkle to Self-Belief: Building a Legacy of Light
By Amy Mandelj 215

A Little Ray of Sunshine
By Gillian Sneddon.. 231

INTRODUCTION

By Anisa Crespo & Natosha Navarro,
Co-Creators of Possibility to Prosperity

When we first said yes to entrepreneurship, we had no idea the journey would require us to break generational patterns, heal wounds we never planned to face, and grow into women we hadn't yet met. We didn't just build businesses—we rebuilt ourselves.

Possibility to Prosperity was born from that transformation. It was born from a promise we made to ourselves—and each other—to stop playing small and start creating a ripple effect of impact and income. A movement where women could rise together, not in competition, but in collaboration.

This book is a collection of stories from women who dared to believe there was more. More purpose. More alignment. More overflow. Women who chose to turn pain into power, purpose into profits, and possibility into real, tangible prosperity.

Each chapter is a mirror. You'll see pieces of your past, your present, and the woman you're becoming.

You'll find hope.
You'll find courage.
And you'll find proof that no matter where you start, you can create a life that feels as good as it looks.

We didn't curate this book to impress you—we curated it to **ignite you**.
To remind you that your story matters. That your voice matters.
And that you are never alone on this journey.

Whether you're just getting started or scaling to new heights, we hope these stories meet you exactly where you are and show you what's possible when you trust the mission placed on your heart.

Welcome to *Possibility to Prosperity*.

Now, let's turn the page—
And start the next chapter of your own transformation.

With love,
Anisa & Natosha

Preface

From the Heart of the Mission

Possibility to Prosperity is more than a book—it's a movement.
It's a testament to what happens when women stop waiting for permission and start choosing themselves.

This collection was created with one mission in mind: to show what's possible when you lead with purpose, rise through adversity, and align your passion with impact. Inside these pages are real stories from women who have lived through loss, self-doubt, fear, and uncertainty—and chose to keep going.

These are not stories of perfection.
They are stories of becoming.

Because success isn't linear. It's layered.
It's messy, miraculous, and deeply personal.
And every woman in this book has walked through her own fire to discover the power she was always meant to embody.

You may not know where your journey will take you, and that's okay.
Neither did we.

What matters is that you're here—reading this—because a part of you knows that you're meant for more. That you were not made to merely survive, but to prosper.

Let these stories light the path.
Let them be the permission slip you've been waiting for.
Let them remind you that you, too, can rewrite your story—starting now.

Welcome to a space where possibility becomes prosperity.
Welcome to your next chapter.

Anisa Crespo

Co-Founder of Million Dollar Mom Society

https://www.linkedin.com/in/anisacrespo/
https://www.facebook.com/anisacrespo
https://www.instagram.com/keepingupwiththecrespos/
https://www.facebook.com/groups/milliondollarmomsociety
https://www.milliondollarmom.org/

Anisa Crespo, Co-Founder of Million Dollar Mom Society, is a powerhouse champion for women's visibility and impact. An Icon of Legacy, Executive Producer and host of Million Dollar Mom Society: The Million Dollar Room docuseries, podcaster, published author, and public speaker, she shares her transformative journey to help other women rise. With a heart for service and a deep sense of purpose, Anisa empowers women to build legacy-driven brands and boldly own their influence. A devoted Mompreneur, twin mom, and woman of faith, she embodies the values of faith, family, freedom, health, and wealth. After walking away from a secure six-figure career, Anisa committed to helping 1,000 Mompreneurs become successful by 2030. As President of Global Women of Impact, she leads with authenticity, creating space for diverse voices and helping women turn their message into movements. Her mission: to illuminate pathways for women to lead, shine, and leave a legacy.

From Scarcity Mindset to Six-Figure Months Through Passion, Purpose, and a Promise to Myself

By Anisa Crespo

The Whisper That Started It All

There are moments in life that shift you so deeply that they don't echo, they roar. But when mine came, it didn't roar at first. It was a whisper. A quiet voice, deep within me, asking:

"Is this really it?"

At the time, I had everything I thought I was supposed to want. A stable job. A house. A family. From the outside, I was "doing well." But inside? I felt like I was living someone else's life. I was chasing checklists that never felt like mine: go to work, smile through the chaos, stretch every dollar, and try not to drown under the weight of being everything for everyone.

Mother. Wife. Employee. Friend.

But nowhere in that list was the one thing I truly needed: **Me.**

The whisper wasn't a breakdown. It was a breakthrough in disguise.

It wasn't telling me to burn my life down but inviting me to rise from within it.

I had spent over a decade in logistics, immersed in a male-dominated industry that rewarded hustle but silenced intuition. I was constantly proving myself in meetings, managing multi-million dollar accounts, and pretending I didn't feel the tug in my soul that kept asking for more... more meaning, more creativity, more heart. I was capable and competent, but I was exhausted from forcing myself to fit a mold that felt misaligned.

The truth is, I was living in my masculine energy 90% of the time, pushing, performing, producing, until I could no longer hear my own voice.

That's when the whisper got louder.

It wasn't from a spreadsheet. It wasn't from my boss.

It was from my spirit.

And it said, "You're here to help women."

At first, that idea felt wild and vague. Help them do what? Start a business? Heal their hearts? Speak their truth? I didn't know the answers. And I didn't need to.

Because one thing I've learned on this journey is that **the how is none of my business**.
My job is to say yes. God takes care of the rest.

What followed was nothing short of a spiritual awakening. I stopped numbing and started listening. I slowed down enough to hear what my body and soul had been trying to tell me for years. I began noticing synchronicities. Women began showing up in my life needing help. Opportunities landed in my inbox that I hadn't even asked for. My faith deepened, my clarity sharpened, and my confidence returned, not because I had a 10-step plan, but because I finally trusted that I didn't need one.

I didn't launch a business. I answered a calling.

And from that calling came community, impact, and abundance.

God and the Universe conspired on my behalf, placing people, mentors, messages, and miracles in my path. Not all at once, but exactly when I needed them. I couldn't have predicted any of it, but I recognized it. Because when you're aligned with your assignment, **doors don't just open, they swing wide**.

I believe so many women hear that same whisper, especially mothers.

We love so deeply that we forget to include ourselves in the equation.

We lose ourselves in the roles we're praised for. But passion doesn't disappear. It simmers.

And when you start listening to it again? That's when everything changes.

I'm not here because I had a perfect strategy.

I'm here because I followed the whisper and trusted the divine to lead the way.

The Breaking Point

You don't reach the breaking point overnight. It's the accumulation of a thousand quiet compromises. The smile when you want to scream. The "yes" when you mean "no." The ignoring of gut feelings, red flags, and the voice inside you begging for more.

For me, it wasn't one thing, it was everything. The pain of unprocessed grief from losing my parents and unborn baby. The guilt I carried from numbing myself through food and substances just to cope with the pressure. The financial chaos, the weight of debt, the constant noise of "you're not enough" that had been playing in my mind for years.

And then... I broke.

But in that breaking, something miraculous happened.

I didn't shatter, I awakened.

I looked in the mirror one morning, eyes tired, heart heavy, and I whispered something different:

"No more."

No more abandoning myself. No more pretending everything was okay. No more settling for survival when I was made for more.

It wasn't easy. Healing never is. But I knew this: I wasn't going to let my children grow up watching their mother shrink. I wanted them to see what it looked like to rebuild. To rise. To rewrite a story in real time.

And that's exactly what I did.

The Rebuild: Faith, Fire, and a Fresh Start

People think rebuilding starts with a business plan. It doesn't.

It starts with the decision to believe in yourself again.

That belief was shaky at first. I had failed before. I had started things and quit. I had made excuses and lived inside stories that weren't even mine. But when I got sober, when I reconnected with my faith, and when I realized I had been living under someone else's definition of "worthy" for far too long, that's when the fire lit inside me.

I began reading books again. Diving into Scripture. Journaling, praying, meditating.

But more importantly, I started dreaming again.

Big, bold, audacious dreams.

Of helping other women. Of building a brand. Of hosting events. Of having a household name. Of creating multiple streams of income that allowed me to build a business without missing out on motherhood.

I created vision boards. I spoke life over my future. I affirmed that I was a vessel, not a victim.

And slowly, that vision turned into plans.

Those plans became offers.

And those offers started bringing in money, lots of money, because they were rooted in authenticity and service.

I stopped asking for permission.

And I started taking aligned action.

How I Turned Passion Into Profit

Let's get practical.

I knew I wanted to help women create freedom and income from home, but that wasn't enough.

I had to figure out how to package that passion into an offer people would actually pay for.

And the secret wasn't in selling. It was in solving.

So, I asked myself the questions that changed everything:

- What do I know that others are struggling with?
- Where have I walked ahead of the women I want to help?
- How can I make their lives easier, lighter, and more profitable?

At first, the answers were simple. I had overcome burnout. I had learned how to show up online even when I was scared. I had built a business without sacrificing my motherhood. So, I started where I was, with a small, humble 1:1 coaching offer at a price point that reflected my confidence at the time.

But what I lacked in polish, I made up for in passion. And results.

My early clients started gaining momentum. They launched offers. They gained clarity. They made sales. They told their friends. And suddenly, I was doing work I loved, and getting paid for it.

That's when I began to create my first digital resources:

- A **checklist** for mompreneurs just starting out
- A **visibility guide** for women scared to show their face online
- **Trainings** on building community through Facebook groups, personal branding, and heart-centered marketing

But I didn't just create offers, I created **experiences**.

I hosted live sessions. I celebrated every win, big or small. I listened deeply. I made every client feel seen, heard, and honored. Because she wasn't just a customer, she was a woman rewriting her life. And that meant everything to me.

As my impact grew, so did my income.

I went from inconsistent $500 months to consistent $5K, $10K... then $20K months. And eventually, my first six-figure month. Not because I had a secret strategy, but because I was finally in alignment, with my mission, my message, and my audience.

But everything shifted to a new level when **Natosha and I joined forces.**

We had both been solo entrepreneurs for years. We had each built successful brands with sheer determination, faith, and grit. But when we met, there was an unmistakable pull, like the Universe was saying, "This is the partnership you've been preparing for."

It didn't take long to realize it was **divine alignment.**

Our strengths complemented each other effortlessly. Our visions mirrored each other. We didn't just collaborate, we **co-created**. And what happened next was exponential.

Our very first offer together was simple, but powerful.

We created a **VIP membership** that helped women in business **get visible** by promoting themselves inside our Facebook group. It gave mompreneurs a platform to be seen, heard, and celebrated. And it worked, fast. Visibility led to momentum. Momentum led to results.

We knew we were onto something.

Next, we began teaching other women how to grow and monetize their own Facebook groups, because that's what we had done. We grew our group rapidly and organically, and it became a goldmine of authentic connection, engaged leads, and high-converting content. We weren't just telling women what to do; we were **showing them, in real time.**

That's when our offer suite began to expand.

We created courses. Coaching programs. Templates. Masterclasses. We launched a membership and then a mastermind. Each new offer was built from lived experience and proven success.

But the real shift came when we began layering in **energetics.**

We realized that strategy alone was never the full answer. Women weren't just stuck because of poor planning; they were stuck because of inner beliefs, nervous system dysregulation, lack of confidence, unhealed trauma, and disconnection from spirit.

So, we integrated it all.

Faith. Energy. Embodiment. Strategy. Execution.

It wasn't hustle, it was **harmonization.**

And we soared.

Our clients weren't just making money, they were becoming **magnetic.**

They were healing, expanding, and reclaiming their power.

They were shifting from "What do I do?" to "Who do I need to be?"

And the answer, always, was: **Your true self.**

That's the secret to profit.

Not just passion, but purpose in motion.

Not just performance, but presence and power.

Not just funnels and ads, but faith, alignment, and energetic truth.

And when you build a business that honors all of you, mind, body, soul, mission...

You don't just succeed.

You soar.

The Rise of the Million Dollar Mom Society

The Million Dollar Mom Society wasn't born from a business meeting or a fancy launch strategy. It was born from a fire in my belly and a promise I made to myself during one of the lowest seasons of my life.

I knew I wasn't the only woman who had ever whispered, "There has to be more than this."

I wasn't the only one trying to break generational cycles while raising babies and rebuilding myself.

And I certainly wasn't the only one tired of being told I had to choose between motherhood and money, nurturing and ambition, and service and success.

So, I built the community I wished existed when I was at my rock bottom.

The Million Dollar Mom Society started with one post. One invitation. One act of courage.

And what happened next still humbles me—women started joining. Fast.

At first, it was a handful of moms who were burned out, overlooked, and stuck in survival mode. Women who were incredibly smart and capable but buried under years of people-pleasing, fear, and false stories of unworthiness.

They came into the group with side hustles, big dreams, or simply a desire to find themselves again.

And together, we built something sacred. A place where faith met strategy, where sisterhood replaced competition, and where women could finally stop hiding and start thriving.

We celebrated every milestone, first $1K day, first coaching client, first live video without fear.

We cried together, laughed together, grew together.

And eventually, the ripple effect began.

Those same moms started becoming leaders. They launched brands, wrote books, built digital courses, got featured in magazines, and even became speakers in our events.

They went from invisible to influential. From depleted to divinely aligned.

The Society didn't just give them tools. It gave them a mirror to see who they really were.

And for me?

It was proof that when you follow purpose and serve with your whole heart, prosperity always follows.

Lessons I Learned Building Multiple Streams of Income

Let me be honest, my first attempts at "multiple streams" looked more like spaghetti thrown at a wall. I had no clue what would work. But I had this deep, unshakable belief that I didn't want to depend on any one thing or person to provide for my family ever again.

So, I started experimenting.

Coaching. Affiliate marketing. Network marketing. Events. Group programs. Digital downloads. E-books. Masterclasses. Partnerships. Media. And eventually, high-ticket mentorship and brand strategy.

Here's what I learned along the way:

1. Visibility is non-negotiable.

No one can hire you if they don't know you exist.

I invested in features, speaking, and getting my story seen. I applied to podcasts, wrote articles, pitched myself for stages, and showed up on social media even when it was scary. Because when you're visible, you become credible.

2. Community converts better than copy.

Yes, messaging matters. But what mattered more was the space I held for women.

The late-night Zoom calls, the voice notes, the realness. That's what made people buy from me. That's what created loyalty and long-term clients.

3. Your past doesn't disqualify you. It prepares you.

Every single hardship I thought discredited me—sobriety, bankruptcy, grief, abuse—it all became part of my unique message. It made me relatable. Human. Trusted.

Because when women see you've walked through fire and still found your light, they believe they can, too.

4. You don't need to do it all alone.

Delegating was hard. I used to think no one could do it like me.

But the truth? Doing it all was keeping me small. The moment I outsourced tasks that drained me, I created space for income-producing activities, and peace.

5. Mindset is the root. Everything else is the fruit.

I've invested in strategy. But the biggest ROI has always come from working on my mind.

My beliefs around money, visibility, God, and success had to evolve before my business ever could.

Once I understood that, I stopped fighting for scraps and started claiming overflow.

From Pain to Platform: Visibility, Impact, and Legacy

There was a time I was terrified to be seen.

I thought if people knew my story, the messy parts, the shameful parts, they wouldn't respect me.

But I've learned that your story is what sets you apart in a sea of sameness.

It's not the polished bio that draws people in.

It's the truth. The transparency. The transformation.

So, I started sharing. Not just the wins, but the wounds.

I shared what it looked like to lose everything and rebuild from nothing.

I shared what it felt like to go live for the first time, to launch a course that flopped, to sell my house, to heal my marriage, to overcome addiction, to make six figures in a month, to be baptized with my husband, to walk fully in my faith.

That realness became my resonance.

And it's what led to the platform I have today. A podcast. A magazine. A brand. A mastermind.

TV shows. Speaking engagements. Opportunities I used to only dream of.

But even with all of that, my definition of success has changed.

It's not just about revenue, it's about ripples.

It's about how many women are now paying it forward because I chose to rise.

It's about legacy.

I want my children to know that their mom didn't just make money, she made moves that mattered.

I want them to see that God can use anyone who says yes.

And I want you to know: if I can do this, so can you.

Stories, Soul, and Success

Success is not just helping women make money, but helping them **remember who they are**.

Helping them walk into rooms they used to shrink in. Helping them activate visions that were once buried under obligation and fear. Helping them break chains their mothers never could.

These moments are the heartbeat of the Million Dollar Mom Society.

It's not just my story, it's a **collective** story.

Women from all over the world are taking what they've lived through and turning it into legacy.

They're healing generational wounds.
They're starting nonprofits.
They're investing in real estate.
They're walking stages and writing books.
They're choosing motherhood and millions.
They're rewriting the rules, and doing it without burning out or burning bridges.

And when I look at my life now, traveling the country, working with my husband, homeschooling our twins, filming a TV show, helping women earn their first (and next) six figures, I often pause to thank the version of me who didn't quit.

The version of me who sent the first email.
Who sold the first $37 offer.
Who posted when nobody liked or commented.
Who cried in the car after the client calls.
Who stayed sober when the temptation crept back in.
Who kept walking in faith when the numbers didn't yet reflect the vision.

Because **she** was the foundation.
And I honor her.
And I honor YOU.

Daily Rituals That Anchored My Rise

Success didn't just come from action; it came from alignment.

Here are a few of the rituals that grounded me while building my empire:

- **Morning Vision Casting**: I would write as if everything I desired had already happened. "Thank you, God, for my

$100K month... for the women I get to serve today... for the podcast interview I'm about to record." This raised my frequency and rewired my mind.

- **Walking in My Future Self**: I stopped dressing, speaking, and showing up like the woman in survival mode. I embodied the Million Dollar Mom version of me even when I still had overdraft notices in my inbox.
- **Power of Proximity**: I intentionally invested in rooms that stretched me. Coaches. Masterminds. Retreats. I sat next to women who were living what I prayed for. And instead of shrinking, I learned.
- **Faith over Force**: Every single time I released control and surrendered to God's timing, better things arrived. I learned to stop striving and start aligning.

Affirmations That Helped Me Stay the Course

You can borrow these anytime you forget who you are:

- I do not chase, I align.
- My story is my strategy.
- Money flows when I lead with service.
- I am the first millionaire in my bloodline, but not the last.
- I am proof that pain births purpose.
- I honor the woman I was, celebrate the woman I am, and believe in the woman I'm becoming.

You Were Built for This

Let me leave you with this:

I'm not special.

I didn't come from wealth. I didn't have a trust fund or an influencer following or a map.

What I had was **resilience**. A dream. And a decision to bet on myself, even when it didn't make sense.

And if you're reading this chapter, I believe it's because something in you is stirring.

Something in you is saying, "It's my turn."

Not just to make money, but to make a mark.

Not just to build a brand, but to build a legacy.

You are not behind.
You are not too late.
You are exactly where you're meant to be.
And the same whisper that once visited me is probably calling to you now.

So take the step.
Launch the offer.
Hire the coach.
Share the story.
Record the podcast.
Go live.
Say yes.

Because your purpose is waiting.
Your clients are waiting.
Your prosperity is waiting.

And I, for one, can't wait to hear your story in the next book.

Your Possibility, Your Prosperity: A Call to Rise

Here's the truth, friend.

You don't need another degree, certification, or perfect business plan.

You don't need to wait until your kids are older, your debt is paid off, or your fear disappears.

You need one thing: the decision to believe that what's inside you is enough to build the life you dream about.

You were not given your story by accident.
You were not called to mediocrity.
You were not created to stay small.

You are a walking permission slip.

When you rise, others rise.
When you heal, others heal.
When you create, others are inspired to create.

This world doesn't need more perfection.

It needs more women who are brave enough to follow the fire in their belly.

So, this is your sign.

This is your sisterhood.

This is your moment.

From scarcity to six-figure months.
From broken to beautifully rebuilt.
From possibility to prosperity.

Let's go.

Natosha Navarro

Co-Founder of Million Dollar Mom Society

https://www.facebook.com/profile.php?id=100093980081725
https://www.milliondollarmom.org/

Natosha Navarro is the co-founder of Million Dollar Mom Society, a community dedicated to empowering women entrepreneurs, particularly moms, to build, grow, and scale their businesses online. With a background in corporate America and a passion for helping women achieve financial freedom, Natosha left her 9-to-5 job after becoming a mother later in life. She co-founded Million Dollar Mom Society alongside her business partner, Anisa Crespo, after discovering the power of digital marketing to create a lifestyle of freedom and flexibility. Today, Natosha helps other ambitious women unlock their potential by teaching them to create irresistible offers, grow engaged Facebook groups, and generate consistent revenue. With a focus on authenticity and strategic growth, Natosha's mission is to guide women to become the entrepreneurs they were always meant to be, without overwhelm. She believes every woman has the ability to create the life and business of her dreams.

Born for More, Built to Rise

By Natosha Navarro

The Mission Was Always There

If you had told me at eight years old that one day I'd write a chapter about walking away from a steady paycheck to chase a dream, I probably wouldn't have laughed. I probably wouldn't have doubted you. I think I would've just nodded and said, "Yeah, I know."

Even then, there was something in me that already understood. I wasn't built for ordinary.

I remember the way the afternoon light filtered through the dusty blinds in my room on base housing. I'd sit cross-legged on the floor with a pile of dolls on one side and pretend business plans on the other, scribbled on lined paper I'd pulled from my school binder. Some girls played house. I played headquarters. I named companies. Assigned fake salaries. Handwrote "CEO" under my name with a crayon. I wasn't trying to be the boss—I just knew I already was.

I used to tell my mom I was going to run my own company. I didn't even fully understand what that meant, but something about it felt like freedom. Not the kind of freedom people throw around in motivational quotes. I mean real freedom—the ability to own my time, to make my own choices, to answer to something bigger than a clock-in or a boss or a policy manual.

Raised for Security, Wired for Freedom

And still, I was raised in a world that deeply valued security. My dad was in the Army. My mom ran our home with strength and steadiness. We moved around a lot—five times by the time I turned eighteen, including a few years overseas in Panama. Change became the only constant. I learned how to read a room fast, make friends quickly but not get too attached, how to adjust and adapt, and smile even when everything inside me wanted to hold onto what I was losing. It made me strong. But it also made me hesitant to fully attach. I didn't realize how deeply that would follow me.

Strength as Armor

That instinct—to stay a little detached, do things myself, not fully let anyone in—followed me. Into adulthood. Into business. Into marriage. Into sisterhood. I confused strength with self-reliance. I wore my independence like armor, not realizing it was keeping me from the very connection I craved. I was good at being capable. I wasn't great at being open.

But awareness is a powerful thing. And over time, I started to notice the walls I'd built. I began to see that the same things that had protected me were now the very things keeping me from expanding. I began to trade control for connection. Surface-level for soul-deep. I started letting people see behind the polished exterior and into the raw, real parts of my story. I learned to soften without losing my power. To be held without being dependent. To lead with more than just logic—I started leading with presence.

Still, even as I unlearned old patterns, one thing never changed: my drive to build.

Building Through Every Season

I've always had side hustles. Even when I was in the military full-time, I was building something after hours. At 21, I started investing in real estate through lease options. I was training clients in the gym before sunrise, teaching spin by lunchtime, and studying contracts and market trends at night. While my peers were heading to happy hour or catching up on sleep, I was reading business books, attending seminars, writing out plans that no one else could see yet. It was exhausting—but it made me feel alive.

The military taught me how to lead, how to follow through, and how to show up no matter what. It also taught me how to armor up, how to perform, and how to operate in a masculine-dominated world without flinching. I learned how to work twice as hard to prove I deserved a seat at the table. And somewhere in that process, I started dimming the softer parts of myself—the intuition, the tenderness, the creative chaos. I became obsessed with performance and proof. I had no idea that the version of me who had built that level of success would eventually need to unravel it all just to find her way home again.

When Success Felt Hollow

Eventually, I transitioned into corporate life. I thought it would feel easier—more stable, less demanding. And in some ways, it was. I had the steady paycheck. The promotions. The perks. I had the team, the schedule, and the status. From the outside, it looked successful. But inside, it felt like something was slowly breaking.

The Breakaway Moment

I remember the moment I realized I couldn't keep doing it. I was sitting in my car in a parking structure, staring at the dashboard with my hands frozen on the wheel. I wasn't sad. I wasn't angry. I was just... numb. Tired in a way that sleep couldn't fix. I thought to myself, *If I go upstairs, I'll smile through another day that chips away at my soul.*

That was the day I let the fear of staying the same finally outweigh the fear of starting over.

So, I left.

I walked away from comfort, status, and stability—and stepped into the unknown. I wrestled with guilt, doubt, and imposter syndrome.

But louder than any of that was my intuition whispering, *This is the way*.

The early days of entrepreneurship weren't graceful. There were nights I'd be nursing my newborn with one arm while typing sales emails with the other. My husband would walk in at 2 a.m. and ask gently, "Are you ever coming to bed?" And sometimes, the answer was no. I was building something. Something that felt bigger than a business plan or a product or a funnel. Something that felt like purpose with a pulse.

It was cold coffee, crying over tech fails, cheering for my first $1K sale. It was messy and unpredictable and deeply personal. It wasn't glamorous. It was gritty. But I wasn't going back.

Motherhood as a Catalyst

Becoming a mother cracked me open in ways I couldn't have predicted. I didn't become a mom until my 40s—after years of infertility, heartbreak, hope, and healing. My first son was born through IVF. My second, to everyone's surprise, arrived naturally. They were miracles, both of them. And they changed the way I saw everything.

Motherhood didn't make me pause. It made me rise.

I vowed to build a life that honored them. I didn't want to be the mom who was always too tired or too resentful or too burnt out to be present. But I also didn't want to lose myself in the process. I wanted them to witness a woman who didn't choose between purpose and presence—but embodied both. That vow became the foundation of everything I've built since.

The DM That Changed Everything

And then, one day, a DM changed everything. A message from a woman named Anisa. What started as a quick hello turned into a

Zoom call, which turned into a conversation about legacy, alignment, and the kind of movement we wished existed for women like us.

Within a few months, Million Dollar Mom Society was born—not as a program, but as a portal. A place where ambitious women could be all of who they are. Where motherhood and money could coexist. Where vision and vulnerability could live in the same room.

Within six months, we hit six figures. By the one-year mark, we had our first six-figure *month*. Then, a six-figure *week*. And soon, we were pacing for a million-dollar month.

The Bold Moves That Changed It All

So how did it happen?

It wasn't luck. It wasn't timing. It wasn't a viral reel or a funnel hack.

It was three bold, aligned, high-stakes decisions:

We invested in ourselves when it didn't make sense.

We said yes to a $100,000 coaching program that stretched every inch of our nervous system. But within 45 days, we'd made our investment back and then some. Because we were finally in the right room. People trusted us faster. We were no longer asking to be seen—we were showing up as leaders. And that decision, wild as it seemed, brought us relationships, access, and a level of visibility we hadn't been able to create on our own.

We stopped relying on strategy and started regulating our energy.

At one point, we were doing everything "right"—but still waking up with tension in our chest. We were burned out, reactive, and disconnected. So, we joined a program that focused entirely on embodiment and energetic alignment. And that one shift changed everything. Suddenly, ease replaced effort. Flow replaced force. We stopped chasing and started magnetizing. We didn't just make more money—we became more ourselves.

We raised our prices—and our standards.

We were doing fine, charging $3,500. But something told us it was time to expand. So we launched $10K, $25K, and even $55K offers. And the wildest part? They sold faster. With less resistance. Because when you raise your prices, you signal to the world that your work carries weight. We stopped overdelivering to prove our value and started owning our worth—fully, boldly, unapologetically.

Of course, we made mistakes. We once signed a 12-month contract with a coach and had to back out three months in. It was embarrassing and humbling. But it also taught us to pause, reflect, and lead with discernment. Now, we stretch with strategy. We invest from alignment, not desperation.

When the Guilt Creeps In

There were moments I wanted to walk away. When launches didn't land. When people criticized what we were building. When the pressure of being a leader felt crushing. And in those moments, my husband—always steady, always supportive—would say, "You don't have to do this. We're okay. You can just stay home."

And just like that, the guilt would slip in—quiet and uninvited—curling around my thoughts like a fog I didn't know how to clear. It whispered questions I thought I'd already answered. Questions that circled me in the stillness of the night and crept into the spaces between mothering and mission. Who chooses pressure when they don't have to? Who builds when she could rest? Who keeps going when no one is asking her to?

But beneath the noise, beneath the pull to justify or explain, there was a deeper knowing—calm, clear, immovable. A knowing that had lived in me since the days I used crayons to draw business plans and believed I could change the world before the world told me to shrink.

What Prosperity Really Looks Like

This was never just about money—not really.

It was about something deeper. Something older. Something that had been flickering quietly in my chest since I was a little girl, sketching business plans in pencil and whispering dreams to the ceiling when no one was listening. It was about honoring that original fire—the one that had always burned steadily, even when the world tried to water it down. Even when I was drowning in algorithms and invoices and responsibilities that didn't leave space for breath, let alone vision. Even when things felt impossible. Even then, the fire stayed.

And now I know it was never about the income. It was always about the intention.

It was about creating a life that allowed me to show my sons—visibly, actively, without apology—that a woman can be both wildly ambitious and profoundly present. That she can lead and nurture, expand and ground, rise and root. That her power is not something she has to trade for love or respect or proximity. That she can hold a microphone one day and a bedtime book the next—and neither makes her more or less of who she truly is.

It was about becoming the version of myself that little me would've looked up to. The version who didn't silence her brilliance to make other people more comfortable. The one who didn't perform for approval or shrink herself for safety. The woman who didn't settle for "just enough" because she had learned to equate sacrifice with virtue.

And now, after years of unraveling old identities and rebuilding from truth, I wake up inside a life that used to feel like fiction.

I get to lead inside rooms I once thought I needed permission to enter. Rooms where women gather not to impress—but to remember. Rooms where one sentence spoken in real truth can change everything. Where we cry and collapse and rise and laugh and strategize and breathe again.

I get to build alongside women who feel like chosen family. Women who are brilliant and brave and raw and real, who speak in vision and walk in faith, who hold me accountable not just to my goals—but to my highest self.

And I get to do it all inside a business that no longer feels like a performance or a persona—but a true extension of my purpose.

This is what prosperity feels like—not just what it looks like.

It's peace in my nervous system, not just numbers on a spreadsheet. It's mornings that begin slow and sacred, where my boys climb into my lap while I sip tea and glance at a calendar I created on my own terms. It's knowing that nothing about this life was handed to me— but that every part of it was *chosen*.

It's coaching women while my toddler plays with dinosaurs at my feet, and my newborn's breath rises and falls beside me. It's creating content with lavender diffusing in the air and candles flickering on the shelf, and a softness in my shoulders I didn't used to know was possible.

It's wealth built from alignment, not burnout. Visibility that expands because it's rooted in service, not shouting. Leadership that no longer feels like pressure to perform—but like an embodied truth that lives in my bones.

It's the kind of prosperity that doesn't drain you. That doesn't ask you to earn rest or prove your worth through constant motion. It's the capacity to pour generously into others without drying out in the process. To give without depletion. To receive without apology. To expand without sacrificing the very things you swore you were building all this for in the first place.

And perhaps the most surprising thing of all—the part no blueprint or business plan can ever fully prepare you for—is how quietly it begins.

The Whisper That Starts It All

It doesn't start with a launch calendar or a funnel.

It doesn't arrive with applause or announcement.

It begins in stillness. In softness. In the kind of silence where your old life starts to feel too small and your future hasn't yet been named.

It begins as a whisper—a barely-there pulse deep in your chest that says, "There's more." More than the tightly drawn lines you've been coloring inside. More than the glass ceiling you were taught to be grateful for. More than the watered-down version of yourself you learned to present just to be palatable, professional, or praised.

More than the survival story you were conditioned to repeat.

And if you feel that whisper now—if you're reading this and something in your body stirs, something ancient and powerful and familiar—you don't have to make sense of it. You don't have to map it out. You just have to *listen*.

Becoming the Brand

Because that sensation in your chest—the one that rises like a swell every time you imagine a life that feels freer, fuller, more honest than the one you're currently living—that isn't delusion. It's not your imagination playing tricks on you or your ambition getting ahead of itself. That ache deep in your belly, the one that tightens when you settle and expands when you daydream, is not a problem to fix. It's a compass to follow. That flicker of energy that sparks behind your eyes when you let yourself—just for a second—believe in the vision you've always held quietly inside you? That's not fantasy.

That's your truth trying to reach the surface.

And it doesn't need to be louder to be real. It just needs to be *trusted*.

You don't need more time—you need to stop negotiating with the clarity that has already made itself known. You don't need a bigger platform, a better plan, or another round of overthinking. You don't need to outsource your confidence to the number of likes, clients, or certificates hanging on your wall. You need to start speaking from the place inside you that you already know. You need to stop waiting to be seen and start acting like you're already visible.

Because the truth is, you are not lacking. You are not behind. You are not unfinished.

You are simply unused to living in full expression.

Your power has never been about perfection. It's not in how polished your content is or how curated your image appears. It's not in how many formulas you follow or how closely you mimic what's worked for someone else. Your power lives in the way you make people feel. In the way you speak what others haven't yet found the words for. In the way you show up raw, real, rooted—in the middle of the mess— and still choose to be seen.

Your magic is not waiting for you at the finish line. It's pulsing through you *right now*. In the questions you're still asking. In the steps you're still afraid to take. In the decision to move forward anyway.

This is the sacred in-between. The stretch between where you are and where you're going. And this, too, is worthy.

So, say yes before the numbers make sense. Raise your prices while your voice still shakes. Write the words that terrify you because they tell the truth. Let your hands tremble on the keyboard, let your palms sweat on stage, let your presence take up space in rooms that weren't built with you in mind—but that are better because you walked in anyway.

Let it be imperfect, not because you're settling—but because you're finally surrendering the lie that perfection is the price of being seen. Let it be inconvenient, because timing will never be ideal and life will never pause long enough for you to feel fully ready. Let it be unpolished, unruly, even a little wild—because the truth doesn't need filters to be felt. Let it be undeniably, unapologetically, unmistakably *yours*.

Because something extraordinary happens the moment you stop auditioning for rooms that were never meant to define you and start choosing yourself with the kind of grounded certainty that doesn't flinch or explain or overcompensate.

The atmosphere around you shifts. Doors you once begged to be opened begin to swing wide without a knock. Paths that once felt foggy begin to appear, illuminated by your own decision to move forward. The right people—the aligned, the resonant, the ones who *see you*—begin to find their way to your work, your words, your world. And in that beautiful unraveling of everything you were taught to be, you find something more sacred than success.

You find *yourself*.

That is the moment you move from potential to embodiment—from the idea of who you could be, to the reality of who you already are when you stop performing and start *owning*.

That is when identity becomes authority—not because someone gave you permission, but because you stopped waiting for it.

That is when you stop shrinking in spaces that can't hold your expansion and start building rooms that reflect the fullness of your voice, your power, your vision.

This Is the Shift

That... that is the moment everything changes.

The moment you stop gripping the edges of survival and begin to rise into the sovereignty that has been waiting for you all along—not because someone finally deemed you ready, but because you finally remembered you always were.

It is the sacred pivot where invisibility fades and your influence begins to stretch across rooms, across timelines, across generations—not through force, but through the quiet, unwavering embodiment of who you really are.

It is the transformation from the flicker of a maybe—the soft, trembling pulse of what *could* be—to the fully realized, breathtaking expression of what *already is* when you stop hiding and let yourself be seen.

This is not just a shift in mindset.

It is a reclamation of identity.

A return to essence.

A homecoming to the truth you've always carried.

And that?

That is exactly what we came here to do.

Jen Conkey

Founder of Legacy Leaders
Life & Business Strategist for Mission-Led Entrepreneurs

https://www.linkedin.com/in/jen-conkey-46190033/
https://www.facebook.com/jennifer.conkey
https://www.instagram.com/jenconkey/
https://www.tiktok.com/@warriorsofwealth_wow

Jen Conkey helps mission-led entrepreneurs earning $450K+ simplify their strategy, clean up execution, and scale with income and impact that match the size of their mission. As the founder of The Legacy Collective, she creates high-performance containers for leaders ready to build with clarity, integrity, and profit.

Known for her no-fluff approach, Jen specializes in uncovering the hidden friction and leaks that quietly drain momentum, and replacing them with clean, scalable execution.

Through her signature War Room intensives and custom 90-day strategies, Jen equips legacy-driven entrepreneurs to move with precision, power, and purpose.

From Shackled to Sovereign: How I Turned Inner Fire Into a Mission-Driven Life

By Jen Conkey

There's a moment when the soul whispers... and you either keep numbing or choose to listen.

Mine came sitting in my car, hands gripped on the steering wheel, staring through a cracked windshield at a life I didn't recognize anymore.

From the outside, things looked fine. I was successful by every conventional measure: a mortgage, a marriage, kids, and a business. I could talk about ROI, business strategy, and checklists like a champ. But inside? I felt like I was bleeding potential. I was slowly suffocating under layers of expectations that weren't mine.

And then one day, I said it out loud:

"This isn't it."

That inner voice was both a breakdown and a breakthrough.

That was the moment my journey from passion to purpose truly began.

I didn't know it at the time, but that whisper in my car was the sound of my soul refusing to be silenced any longer. It wasn't a dramatic awakening; it was more like a subtle cracking open. But that crack? That was how the light finally got in. I had spent so long building a life I thought I should want, I had forgotten how to ask what I actually desired. The question, "What do I truly want?" became my daily compass.

Phase One: The Shackles We Don't See

I didn't set out to become a mindset mentor, a transformational leader, or a retreat host. I set out to survive. To provide. To be impressive enough to matter. And I got really, really good at building a life that looked perfect on paper but felt hollow in my soul.

We're not taught to recognize shackles when they come dressed as trophies. But that's exactly what they were-golden handcuffs made of performance, perfectionism, and pressure.

Some of the shackles were external:

- Systems that rewarded output over well-being.
- Social narratives that told me being "too much" would make me unlovable.
- Praise I got for being busy, not for being whole.

But the heaviest shackles were the ones I forged in my own mind.

The voice that said, "You have to prove your worth."

The belief that said, "If you slow down, it will all fall apart."

The lie that whispered, "There's no room for your softness here."

Naming them was the first act of liberation.

I tell my clients this all the time:

> *"You can't shift what you won't face. And you can't heal*
> *what you refuse to name."*

In the stillness of those moments when I stopped long enough to hear my own heartbeat, I realized I was living a version of success that required me to abandon myself.

Phase Two: Rewriting My Identity

Once I saw the shackles, I couldn't unsee them. But awareness without action just becomes another layer of guilt. So, I had to choose from keep betraying myself, or start becoming who I really am.

This part wasn't glamorous. It didn't involve a rebrand or a viral quote. It was awkward, humbling, and often invisible to anyone watching from the outside.

I started rewriting my identity in small, defiant ways:

- I stopped taking clients that drained me.
- I built white space into my calendar, not for productivity, but for presence.
- I made peace with disappointing people who weren't aligned with my evolution.

I realized something radical:

I didn't need to burn everything down to find my purpose. I just had to stop abandoning myself in the name of "success."

It was around this time that I started asking deeper questions. Not what do I want to do, but who do I want to become?

The answers came in the quiet. They came through journaling, breathwork, stillness, movement, and sacred conversations. They came when I finally stopped outsourcing my power and started trusting the voice within.

> *"Passion isn't always loud. Sometimes, it's a quiet ache that refuses to die."*

I took that ache and I built something sacred.

That "something sacred" didn't come from a five-step plan. It came from a daily devotion- from crying on the yoga mat, from voice notes to myself, and from building offers that felt like soul assignments instead of just sales pages. I began building a life and business that felt like art, messy, intuitive, alive. I wasn't chasing some polished ideal. I was creating from the inside out. And as I became more of me, my community started rising with me. That's when I knew I wasn't just personal but collective.

Phase Three: From Hustle to Harmony

There's this belief that high performance and high peace are mutually exclusive, that the only way to build something powerful is to break yourself in the process. That belief nearly broke me.

I was addicted to checking boxes and outrunning the fear of "not enough."

But purpose doesn't bloom from burnout. It blooms from alignment.

So, I started asking a new question:

"What would it look like to build from a regulated nervous system?"

That question changed everything. It became the basis for the Time Mastery Blueprint I now teach in my programs.

Here's what I learned:

- Hustle is a trauma response.
- Urgency is not the same as clarity.
- Just because you can doesn't mean you should.

In this phase, I began restructuring my days not around how much I could squeeze in, but around how deeply I could feel and how clearly I could move.

I designed my life with intention:

- Morning rituals that grounded me before the world could distract me.

- 90-day goals rooted in purpose, not performance.
- Strategic rest that fueled creative fire.

I wasn't just optimizing time, I was reclaiming my energy.

Phase Four: Making Shift Happen

The moment I stopped treating business like a transaction and started treating it like a sacred vehicle for transformation, that's when everything changed.

I stopped selling tactics. I started creating spaces - where women could finally exhale; and where they could lay down the armor and pick up their truth.

One woman came to me completely burnt out -a high performer, successful on paper, but spiritually bankrupt. Through our work together, she didn't just restructure her business; she restructured her beliefs. She reconnected to joy. She launched a new brand aligned with her soul. And most importantly, she started living again.

That's what this is about.

Not just helping people scale their businesses, but helping them scale their capacity for joy, wealth, connection, and self-trust.

> *"My goal isn't to help you make more money.*
> *It's to help you make more meaning with the money you*
> *make."*

The spaces don't need to be always physical. Sometimes, they're Zoom rooms filled with tears and truth. Sometimes, they're Voxer threads with voice messages that sound more like prayers. Other times, they're silent moments where someone finally breathes for the first time in years.

Transformation doesn't need flashing lights; it needs safety, intention, and deep listening.

And that's the work I committed to: Creating containers where women can unlearn the noise and remember their essence. Because once a woman hears her true voice again? She becomes a wildfire of impact and embodiment .

Phase Five: Building a Movement

Eventually, this became bigger than me.

I wasn't just creating coaching containers, I was birthing a movement.

That movement now lives inside The Ascension Retreats. These aren't spa weekends. These are soul initiations.

At The Ascension, we blend strategy with shadow work. We laugh, we cry, we unlearn. Women show up one way, and leave unrecognizable to the version of themselves they once thought was their only option.

Yes, we work on business structure, offer creation, and strategic scaling.

But we also do breathwork. Cold plunges. Sound healing. Deep mindset rewiring.

We talk about generational trauma and generational wealth in the same breath, because both live in the body, and both deserve your attention.

These retreats are where possibility meets prosperity, where we burn the old blueprint and draw up a new one... one that honors your full self, not just the parts that perform.

These retreats are designed to disrupt comfort zones with love and precision. The women who come are not beginners; they're powerful, accomplished, and often secretly exhausted. They're leaders, mothers, coaches, and entrepreneurs. And they're ready to stop living fractionally.

At The Ascension, we strip it all back. We meet shame. We rewrite old scripts. We reconnect to the body. We dream bigger, then build the infrastructure to hold those dreams.

Women leave with strategies, yes, but they also leave with a new nervous system, a new voice, and a new standard. It's not about changing their life for a weekend. It's about changing their energetic frequency for good.

Phase Six: Creating Wealth That Circulates

I call myself a Wealth Circulator for a reason.

Wealth is not just about accumulation; it's about circulation.

It's not about hoarding. It's about having more than enough so you can give, invest, and transform lives, starting with your own.

Wealth is:

- The ability to take a Tuesday off just because you want to.
- The freedom to say no to clients who aren't aligned.
- The power to write checks that change someone else's trajectory.
- The energetic stability to build from overflow, not urgency.

Circulation is the model.

Because when a woman reclaims her power and her profit, she becomes unstoppable. And more importantly, she becomes generous.

I teach my clients not just how to earn more, but how to hold more, circulate more, and become a vessel for impact.

Lessons from the Black Swan

My brand symbol is a black swan.

Why?

Because black swans are rare. Unexpected. They symbolize disruption, mystery, and transformation. They don't follow. They don't shrink. And when they arrive, they alter the landscape.

You are a black swan, too.

If you've ever felt out of place in the rooms you once dreamed of...

If you've ever felt like your dreams were "too much" for people who settled for less...

If you've ever wondered if there was something wrong with you because you want more, not just different...

You're not broken.

You're a black swan. You were never meant to fit the mold.

You were meant to create a new one.

You're not meant to blend in; you're meant to blaze a trail so bright that others find their way through your fire.

That's the power of becoming a Black Swan. It's not just about being rare. It's about being unapologetically whole.

The world needs your edges, your softness, your story, your leadership.

You don't have to be louder. You just have to be truer.

The Framework That Created Everything

Everything I teach lives inside a simple but powerful framework:

1. Awareness

Get honest. Name the patterns. Identify the internal (and external) shackles that are keeping you playing small.

2. Alignment

Get clear. Define your next-level vision. Embody the identity of the woman who already lives it. Speak like her. Move like her. Decide like her.

3. Action

Get moving. But not from urgency, from embodiment. Build a 90-day plan rooted in aligned execution. Focused. Strategic. Sacred.

Every major life pivot I've made came from frequently working this framework.

> *"Awareness without alignment is anxiety.*
> *Alignment without action is fantasy.*
> *Action without awareness is burnout."*

But when all three are activated? That's how you become sovereign.

Final Thoughts: You Are the Shift

If you've read this far, you already know that:

Something inside you is stirring. A deeper truth is calling. A bigger life is trying to get your attention.

Don't ignore it.

The world doesn't need more women who can follow instructions.

It needs more women who are willing to remember who they are... and rise.

You don't have to burn your life down to begin again.

You just have to stop betraying yourself to impress.

Start small. Follow what feels alive.

Say yes to what gives you breath. Say no to what takes it away.

Your shift doesn't have to be loud. But it does have to be true.

You don't need permission normore credentials.

You don't need to wait for the right moment.

You are the moment.

You are the wealth.

You are the spark.

> *"The door is open.*
> *You've always had the key.*
> *The shift is about to go down… are you ready?"*

With love, fire, and fierce belief in you,
Jen Conkey
Life & Business Strategist, Speaker, Author, and Wealth Circulator
"Shifts About To Go Down"

Stacy Conkey

Remote Multifamily Investing Academy
Founding Partner

https://www.linkedin.com/company/she-rises-studios/
https://www.facebook.com/sherisesstudios
https://www.instagram.com/sherisesstudios_llc/
www.SheRisesStudios.com

Stacy Conkey is a globally respected multifamily real estate investor, capital strategist, and transformational mentor known for helping ambitious professionals build wealth that lasts for generations.

As the Founding Partner of the Remote Multifamily Investing Academy, Stacy equips investors with the tools, structure, and strategic guidance to create scalable, diversified portfolios—no matter where they live. Her mission is to remove the overwhelm, demystify the process, and make real estate investing accessible, aligned, and deeply profitable.

Her personal holdings are a powerful testament to her expertise, spanning multifamily assets, single-family homes, mobile home parks, a boutique motel, Airbnbs, and even a revenue-generating RV. In addition to owning and operating these assets, she's also a partner in two debt fund companies and co-founder of Capital Titans, a capital raising firm that connects accredited investors with high-yield, highly aligned opportunities that generate both income and impact.

With over two decades of experience, Stacy is known for her rare blend of no-BS strategy, bold clarity, and deep purpose. She doesn't just teach passive income—she ignites transformation. Her coaching and programs help high-performing professionals transform fear into focused action and scale their portfolios without burnout, confusion, or costly mistakes.

Stacy is not only an investor—she's a movement-maker. She helps her clients claim financial sovereignty and step into legacy-level wealth building with intention, confidence, and control. Through her signature methods and sharp strategic insight, she's redefining what's possible in the world of real estate investing and capital strategy.

If you're ready to stop playing small and start building real, lasting wealth on your own terms, Stacy Conkey is the one to learn from.

Never Again

By Stacy Conkey

This is the raw, unfiltered story of how I went from fighting through setbacks and obstacles to discovering a passion that not only rebuilt my life, but gave me the freedom and security I never thought possible.

There was a time I didn't believe financial freedom was possible for me.

Like everyone else, I was working hard, playing by the "rules," and still ending most months wondering...

Is this really all there is?

I thought life would look different.

What's the point of all of this?

I wasn't lazy. I wasn't unmotivated.

But I was stuck.

Thankfully, somewhere in the middle of all that chaos, I stumbled onto something that would change everything. A path that started as curiosity, grew into a passion, and ultimately became my way not just to survive but to thrive.

That path? Small multifamily real estate.

Not the skyscraper-size apartment complexes you see in glossy magazines. I'm talking about 4-unit buildings, 12-unit buildings, 25-unit buildings properties that real people like you and me can own.

And here's the part most people miss:

They produce a steady cash flow month after month.

They come with tax benefits that can erase (or even reverse) your tax bill.

They create passive income you don't have to clock in for.

They can fund your retirement and build generational wealth.

It's almost 17 years later that I'd step in and help people skip the years of mistakes, fear, anduncertainty I went through, and go straight to building the life they want. In January 2020, the Remote Multifamily Investing Academy was established.

The story to the path I took of how I got here is not a straight line. It's not always pretty far from it, actually. But it's real. And if there's one thing I hope you take away from it, it's that even when the odds are stacked against you, possibility can turn into prosperity.

It was June 10, 2003, and Alaska was gorgeous with cold, crisp air. Glaciers standing like silent Sentinels. For a week, I'd been off the grid with my family on a cruise, a rare break from my role as a Controller for a public company. The CFO had been ousted by the board just months earlier.

And while the title was empty, I'd been doing the work, running the company alongside the CEO and COO, working on my master's degree, forcing myself to learn public speaking (even though it made me want to hurl), and building a case to earn that CFO title outright.

I was 28 and on the corporate track I thought would lead to "success."

The safe track.

The secure track.

The one you're told will guarantee the dream.

That illusion ended that day.

We were stepping off the ship for a day in port when my phone came alive.

Ding.

Ding.

Ding.

A rapid-fire barrage of text notifications...so many, so fast, it sounded unnatural. My family was smiling, laughing, ready for adventure. For me, the nightmare had just begun as the blood drained from my face. The sound around me seemed warped, like I was underwater.

Their voices came through like echoes from another dimension:

"What's wrong? Stacy? Are you okay?"

I couldn't speak. I couldn't breathe. My stomach clenched. My hands shook.

The messages were from my staff-frantic, desperate. The board had just fired the CEO and

COO. Two men I trusted. Two men I knew had impeccable integrity.

And I knew exactly why they were gone.

The board wanted their guy back, the shady former CEO who had treated the company like his personal piggy bank. They wanted the perks, the excess, the corruption.

In that moment, one truth smacked me dead in the face:

There is no such thing as a safe job.

The story I'd been sold my whole life - go to college, work hard, climb the ladder, retire comfortably was complete BS. A fabricated model of "security" that collapses the second someone above you decides your time is up.

I had no savings. No backup plan.

And the certainty I'd built my life on - the job, was gone in an instant.

Standing there on that dock, I realized I was just a puppet on someone else's strings. And I made myself a promise: *Never again*.

Never again would my survival depend on the whims of a boardroom. Never again would my well-being rest in the hands of people whose values I didn't share. That day, my mindset did a 180. I didn't know exactly how yet, but I knew this: I would figure out how to make a living on my terms. First, through independent business consulting.

Eventually, through real estate investing, where passive income could replace a boss, a board, and the constant fear that the rug could be yanked out from under me.

That day wasn't just the end of an illusion.

It was the day my entrepreneurial journey began.

From a mindset standpoint, I was solid.

Yes! I can do this! I must do this!

And for about five minutes, that belief was enough to make me feel invincible.

But here's what they don't tell you about walking away from a "safe" paycheck: The adrenaline rush wears off a whole lot faster than the panic. On paper, my decision looked bold, courageous, and maybe even glamorous. But in real life? I was a walking ball of nausea. My appetite vanished for months. I lost weight without trying, not because I had discovered some miracle diet, but because my stomach was in such a constant knot of fear I could barely choke down a cracker. It's the best weight loss plan I would never recommend.

Everywhere I turned, people thought I'd lost my mind. Friends smiled at my face, but had "concerned" conversations about me the minute I left the room. Some didn't bother to whisper; they told me straight out I was being reckless and irresponsible. Which, honestly, was ridiculous.

I have a four-year business degree in accounting. I'd spent two years as an auditor for one of the Big 5 accounting firms. I had my CPA license. Numbers were my second language. Analysis was my middle name. I didn't make moves based on wishful thinking. I ran the data. And the data was screaming at me: The biggest risk was staying where I was.

The truth had been exposed, and I couldn't unsee it. The "safe job" myth was shattered. I'd been handed the red pill and the blue pill, and I'd swallowed the red pill. There was no going back to life in the haze.

I knew this:

If I stayed in that false sense of security, I would forever be one boardroom decision away from financial collapse. That wasn't a life. That was a hostage situation.

So I made the decision. The kind that feels less like a leap and more like setting fire to the bridge behind you. No more letting someone else hold the strings. No more putting my survival in anyone else's hands. It was time to stop being the victim of circumstance and start being the architect of my own future.

The Three Freedoms

When I walked away from that so-called "safe" corporate path, I didn't have language for what I was chasing. I just knew I wanted control.

Not just over my paycheck.

Not just over my calendar.

Over my life.

It wasn't until years later, after the panic, after the steep learning curves, after finally cracking the code on small multifamily investing, that I could name them. I was after the *Three Freedoms*.

Money Freedom

It is the ability to generate income that isn't capped by an employer or tied to how many hours I could work.

In my corporate days, my salary looked good on paper until you realized it came with a glass ceiling you couldn't shatter without someone else's permission. With small multifamily properties, that ceiling disappeared. My cash flow could grow as much as I was willing to grow it - one property at a time. Rent checks didn't care if it was Tuesday at 2:00 PM or on a Sunday morning. And the tax benefits? They made me wonder why this wasn't taught in every high school in America.

Time Freedom

This one hit me unexpectedly. In the beginning, I thought time freedom meant not having to clock in at an office. But it's deeper than that. It's waking up and knowing you decide how your day unfolds. Today, it's being at my kids' events without having to ask for time off. It's blocking a random Wednesday for a hiking trip because the weather's perfect. It's also doing focused work when my energy is high, instead of forcing myself into someone else's schedule.

Location Freedom

This one is addictive. When you run your investments the right way, you can manage them from anywhere. I've closed deals from coffee shops in different states, reviewed renovation progress from a beach in Mexico, and even handled tenant communications while on the sidelines of my kid's soccer game. It's the freedom to choose - to live where you want, travel when you want, and know your income comes with you.

At first, I thought these freedoms were luxuries for "other people." People richer than me, braver than me, luckier than me. Turns out, they were simply the byproducts of building the right kind of assets, and being willing to push through the discomfort to get there. That's the gift real estate gave me: A life I didn't need a vacation from. And eventually, the privilege of showing others how to get there faster than I did.

Turning Passion into Profit

When I first stepped into real estate investing, I thought I was buying my ticket to freedom. Instead, I bought a $40,000-lesson on how to light money on fire. The "education" I paid for looked shiny from the outside - glossy brochures, confident presenters, and the promise that investing was "easy if you just follow our steps." But once they had my check? It was all smoke and mirrors. No real strategies. No real support. No one who seemed to have actually done what they were Teaching. And that "simple step-by-step" they promised? It was like being handed a treasure map with half the landmarks missing.

So I learned the hard way.

I hit my head on every branch of the real estate learning tree - bad contractors, nightmare tenants, deals that bled cash instead of producing it. But through the bumps and bruises, I started to figure out something that actually worked.

I discovered that starting with small multifamily properties that were generally between 2-20 units were the sweet spot, particularly when getting started. For the first time in my life, I could see a direct connection between my actions and my financial security. And that was exhilarating!

Then something unexpected happened.

People started asking me for help. At first, it was friends and fellow investors: "Hey, can you look at this deal?" Then it became: "Can you show me exactly how you're doing this?"

When I walked them through my process, their results came faster than mine ever had. They avoided the mistakes that had slowed me down. And I realized... *I loved this.* I loved the lightbulb moments. I loved breaking complex ideas down so clearly that even someone brand new could feel confident taking action. People kept telling me, "No one explains it like you do."

That's when I got it:

When you've fought your way through the jungle, some people want you to hand them the machete and point them toward the shortcut while walking alongside them. And more than that...the world needed me. They needed someone who would teach it all. Not just the highlight reel. Not just the fluff. But the real how-to, with all the messy, unfiltered parts included.

Because here's the truth: Most people, if they had to go through what I went through, would quit. They'd toss their dreams in the trash and crawl back to their so-called "safe" life. And I couldn't let that happen. That's when my passion ignited.

I didn't set out to be a coach. I didn't plan to find my purpose in teaching. But it found me.

Real estate investing gave me the skills. Teaching gave me my purpose. And together, they became the foundation of the Remote Multifamily Investing Academy where I started taking people from "I don't know where to start" to "I just closed my first deal," without them wasting years or losing tens of thousands like I had.

Building the Engine

Once I realized I had a process that worked, I did what any numbers nerd with a CPA license would do - I reverse-engineered it. I didn't want a business that ran on luck. I wanted a machine. So I pulled apart every deal I'd done, the wins and the disasters, and started looking for atterns - What had to happen first to avoid chaos later? Where were the hidden landmines?

Which steps gave me the biggest returns?

I came up with a clear, repeatable framework for buying multifamily properties that could be run from anywhere, by anyone willing to follow the system. And here's what made it different from all the $40,000 "fluff" program I'd wasted my money on: It wasn't theory. It wasn't smoke and mirrors. It wasn't recycled content from a guru who hadn't bought a property in years. It was field-tested - built from the trenches, not a conference stage. And because I'm a stickler for results, I tested my framework over and over on my own deals and on my students'.

The result?

Predictable success.

The best part? My students were buying their first deals in months, not years. They weren't paralyzed by overthinking or drowning in conflicting advice. I'd built a business engine that did what my $40,000 "education" never did:

It actually worked.

And once that engine was running smoothly for me, it became the heart of the Remote Multifamily Investing Academy - the thing that turned my passion for teaching into a scalable business, and my own portfolio into the foundation for the freedom I live today.

The Lifestyle Shift

Looking back on my early days, I'll never forget the first morning I woke up and realized, *I didn't have to be anywhere.*

No alarm blaring at 6 AM.

No email inbox screaming for attention.

No boardroom waiting to decide my fate.

Just quiet. And the freedom to choose.

That's when it hit me. I'd built a life I didn't need to escape from. The crazy thing? The deeper I stepped into this life, the more I wanted to pull others into it with me. Because I know what it feels like to: Sit in a cubicle and wonder if this is all there is. Smile through the exhaustion because you're too afraid to admit you're burned out. Have your "security" pulled out from under you in an instant.

And I know the rush of signing the papers on your first property. The thrill of watching rent checks roll in. The moment you realize you'll never have to beg for a raise again. This isn't just about property.

It's about possibility.

And because I'd lived on both sides of the panic and the prosperity, I couldn't help but want everyone, too, to taste the freedom I had found.

A Direct Challenge

So here's a question.

If nothing changes in your life right now, where will you be five years from today?

Still clocking in for a job that could vanish overnight?

Still trying to convince yourself that exhaustion is "normal"?

Still hoping someone else will give you permission to live the life you want?

Here's the raw, no BS truth:

There is no perfect time.

There is no magic guarantee.

There is only the choice to step out of the comfort zone and into the arena.

When I left my corporate job, I didn't have all the answers. I didn't even know all the questions.

But I knew one thing: Staying put was far riskier than the uncertainty of change. That's the real turning point. When the pain of staying the same outweighs the fear of doing something different.

So what about you?

Are you going to keep telling yourself "someday"? You don't need to have it all figured out. You just need to decide that you're done living in the haze. hat you're ready to see what's on the other side of the red pill.

And when you do, you'll discover something powerful:

Prosperity isn't for "other people." It's for those willing to claim it.

Closing Vision

I think back to that day in Alaska often. I remember the panic, the nausea, the weight of realizing the "safe" life I'd built was nothing but smoke and mirrors.

But here's the thing. If I could go back and stand next to that terrified version of me on the dock, I wouldn't change a thing. Because that was the day I woke up. That was the day I stopped waiting for permission. That was the day I decided to bet on myself.

Today, my life looks nothing like it did back then. I own my time, my income, and my location. I've built a business that helps hundreds of other people create the freedom they've been craving.

And it all started with one impossible-to-ignore truth:

No one is coming to save you.

But when you decide to save yourself? When you take that first shaky step toward possibility? That's when the door to prosperity swings open.

I didn't just find a way to invest in property.

I found a way to invest in people - myself first, then the students who trusted me to guide Them. And now, every time I watch someone close on their first property, every time I hear, "I quit my job today," I'm reminded of something powerful: We don't just build portfolios. We build lives.

So here's my closing vision for you:

Imagine waking up five years from now and realizing you don't have to go anywhere unless you want to. Your bills are paid before you pour your first cup of coffee. You can choose to work from a beach, a cabin, or your own backyard. You're no longer surviving - you're designing.

It's not a fantasy.

It's what happens when you decide that your life is defined by possibility, and have the courage to turn it into prosperity.

Thyra Newby

Founder of Live Life Empowered Coaching

https://www.linkedin.com/in/thyra-newby
https://www.facebook.com/ThyraNewby
https://www.facebook.com/groups/traumatotriumph2025
https://www.youtube.com/@LiveLifeEmpowered
https://www.livelifeempoweredcoaching.com

Thyra Newby is a Certified Transformational Life Coach, International Best-Selling Author, and resilient advocate dedicated to helping others reclaim their voice, break generational cycles, and live with purpose. Featured in Hispanic Stars Rising V, a #1 Amazon best-seller, and in the international best-seller Transforming Pain into Purpose: Tales of EmpoweHERment, Vol. 3, she shares her powerful journey of healing and self-discovery to inspire others to rise above adversity and step boldly into their own empowerment. She volunteers as a Resident Advocate at a domestic violence and sexual assault center, providing compassionate support to survivors during their most vulnerable moments. Her passion for advocacy is rooted in lived experience, fueling her mission to help others find strength in their stories. Thyra holds a Bachelor's in Business Management with a minor in Psychology, an MBA in Human Resources and Organizational Behavior, and a post-graduate certificate in Psychology Studies. Outside of work, she enjoys traveling with her husband, sharing meaningful moments with her daughter and bonus sons, and spending time with her beloved Boston Terrier.

I Am the Possibility:
From Silence to Sovereignty

By Thyra Newby

I was born in Manhattan, New York, right into the chaos and heartbeat of a city that never sleeps. But don't let the skyline fool you. My childhood was not one of flashing lights or luxury. It was poverty. It was struggle. And it was survival.

By the time I was a little girl, our family had moved to Puerto Rico, where we quickly learned that survival had a different rhythm. The beauty of the island was undeniable: the golden sun, the chorus of coquí frogs at night, the scent of mangos so ripe they practically fell off the trees. But those mangos weren't just tropical luxuries. They were our meals.

We climbed trees to eat.

That wasn't a metaphor. It was our reality. If we wanted to eat that day, we had to get creative. Mangos, avocados, quenepas, whatever the land gave us, we were grateful. Hunger made us resourceful. It made us inventive. And it planted the first seeds of resilience in me. I didn't have the words for it back then, but I was already learning to fight for my life.

Even as a child, I knew: I would have to become my own possibility.

We returned to New York eventually, this time to the Bronx. And if Puerto Rico had taught me to be resourceful, the Bronx taught me to be alert. Salsa music spilled out of windows, Spanglish conversations bounced through the stairwells, and life felt fast and hard. Our apartment was ice-cold in the winter and suffocating in the summer. Poverty followed us back to the States, wearing a different outfit but the same weight.

My childhood was marked by moments that should never happen to a child. I was sexually assaulted by people who were supposed to protect me. And when I looked around for safety, there wasn't much. My mother was raising five of us on her own, doing her best, but I often felt like I was navigating a dark maze by myself.

And yet, somewhere deep in that chaos, something inside me said: This isn't where your story ends.

When we moved to Miami, it was supposed to be a fresh start. But poverty packed itself in our luggage. The struggle continued. Beans and rice became our go-to meal, stretched to fill more stomachs than it should have. I wore homemade clothes stitched by my mother and me. My shoes told the story of years walked too soon. School wasn't a refuge; it was another battlefield. Kids can be cruel, and poverty made me a target.

Still, I held a quiet, stubborn hope.

There were nights I sat by the ocean, looking out at the endless horizon, dreaming that one day I'd cross it, not just physically, but emotionally, mentally, and spiritually. I didn't want just to survive. I wanted to rise.

That desire to rise carried me into young adulthood. But the climb wasn't linear. I fell into a violent relationship as a teenager. He hit me. He broke more than my skin. He shattered the last bit of belief I had in my worth.

Until one day, I looked in the mirror. My face was swollen. My eyes were tired. But something fierce woke up in me.

"I deserve better," I whispered.

I left. And then, he stalked me. For months. One night, he found me in a car with a friend. He pulled up beside us with a rifle. Pulled the trigger. My friend was killed in front of me. The car crashed. I blacked out.

When I came to, my friend was slumped over the steering wheel. His blood on my skin. Brain matter in my hair. I stumbled out of that car on hands and knees, banging on the nearest apartment door. A stranger let me in. I curled up in the corner, shaking, soaked in trauma.

Police surrounded me like a human shield. That night should have broken me.

But it became the night I decided to fight for my life.

I didn't become whole overnight. Grief gutted me. Guilt consumed me. There were nights I cried so hard I thought my body would fold in on itself. Nights where sleep wouldn't come, only flashbacks and whispers of everything I had lost. My mind was a storm of "what-ifs" and "if-onlys." I questioned everything: my choices, my worth, my ability to move forward. It felt like I was drowning in a grief no one could see.

But slowly, I began to rebuild.

I found a trauma therapist who saw me, all of me. She didn't try to fix me. She didn't speak in platitudes. She listened. She held space for the parts of me that had never been held before. She helped me remember who I was before the pain and showed me how to reclaim that girl. We talked. We journaled. We cried. We used EMDR. We unearthed wounds that had been buried so deep I forgot they were even mine. But with each session, I felt a little lighter.

Bit by bit, I reclaimed my voice. Not the one that whispered for permission, but the one that roared with truth.

I started volunteering at domestic violence shelters, sitting with other women, sharing stories that mirrored my own. I looked into their eyes and saw pieces of myself. I let them borrow my hope until they found their own. We weren't victims. We were warriors with bruised armor, standing in solidarity, not shame.

That was the moment I realized: My pain had a purpose.

Possibility re-entered my life quietly.

At first, possibility felt unfamiliar. It didn't roar, it whispered. It showed up in late-night Google searches about trauma recovery, in journaling sessions where I wrote until my hand cramped, in self-help books with dog-eared pages and tear stains. Possibility was me showing up for myself every day, even when no one else did. It was messy. It was private. But it was sacred.

It looked like going back to school. First, my bachelor's degree. Then, my MBA. I remember the night I finished my last MBA assignment. I was in the kitchen, in sweatpants, with my laptop glowing beside a pot of simmering pollo guisado. I hit "submit" and just started crying. Not because it was hard, but because I had done it. A girl who once relied on school lunches to get through the day had just earned her master's degree. I wasn't just achieving. I was reclaiming every lost part of myself.

It looked like telling my story in published books. It looked like launching my coaching business, Live Life Empowered, so other women could break free, too.

The idea for my coaching business was born out of heartbreak and hard-won healing. I remember sitting in front of my computer with trembling hands, wondering if anyone would care about what I had to say. But the truth is, we don't coach from perfection; we coach from experience. Every scar and stumble became part of the curriculum I now use to help others rewrite their own stories. My first client cried during our session, not because of pain, but because for the first time, she felt seen.

That moment cracked something open in me. I realized this work wasn't just about helping others heal; it was helping me remember who I was called to be. Every story I listened to felt sacred. Every breakthrough felt like divine confirmation. Coaching wasn't a job. It was purpose woven from pain. I no longer needed anyone else's permission to lead. I was already qualified—by experience, by empathy, by grace.

I didn't become a coach and mentor to impress anyone. I became a coach and mentor because I knew what it felt like to drown in silence, to ache for someone who truly understood. Every woman I work with is a reflection of the woman I used to be: unsure, overextended, underestimated. And every session is sacred. Not because I have all the answers, but because I've walked through the fire and came out carrying buckets of water for those still burning.

I remember one client, a woman in her 40s, who came to me with a trembling voice and years of self-doubt. She'd been the caregiver, the fixer, the family sponge absorbing everyone else's pain. When I asked her what she wanted—not what she needed, not what she should do, but what she truly wanted—she froze. Weeks later, she sent me a message: "I told my family no for the first time. I didn't over-explain. I didn't feel guilty. I just said no. And I meant it." I sat there holding that message, tears in my eyes, knowing this is the work that changes lives.

And it looked like love.

Real love. The kind that doesn't hurt. The kind that holds you steady and celebrates your shine. My husband walked into my life when I was learning to walk again emotionally. He didn't rescue me. He honored me. With his support, I learned boundaries. I learned rest. I learned joy.

My bonus sons, my daughter, and our little dog? They are my prosperity. They are the proof that cycles can be broken. That love can be rewritten.

So, what does prosperity mean to me?

It means peace. The kind that hums in your chest when no one is watching.

It means impact. Hearing a client say, "You helped me find my voice."

It means freedom. To rest. To create. To love myself unapologetically.

It means writing my story, not to relive it, but to release it. To offer it as a roadmap to the woman still sitting in silence. The one reading this with tears in her eyes at 2 a.m., wondering if her life can ever change.

It means waking up and knowing you are living a life that reflects your values, not anyone else's expectations.

Let me say this to her:

Yes. It. Can.

Lessons from the Climb:

1. You don't owe anyone your silence. For too long, I thought staying quiet was keeping the peace. But peace built on silence isn't peace at all.
2. Boundaries are bridges to your freedom. They don't shut others out; they protect your power.
3. Healing is not linear. There are days you'll feel like you've gone backwards. You haven't. You're resting.
4. Being the family scapegoat was a sacred redirection. It showed me who I was never meant to become.
5. You can start over at any age. I got my MBA later in life. I launched my business after years of being unseen. The only deadline is the one you create.
6. Imposter syndrome is a liar. Just because you hear the voice of doubt doesn't mean you have to believe it.
7. You don't have to explain your healing to people who are committed to misunderstanding you.

This is prosperity.

Prosperity is when your life reflects your truth.

It's watching a woman you coach stand up to generational shame for the first time.

It's seeing your face on a billboard in Times Square and realizing the girl who used to climb trees to eat now helps women climb out of emotional cages.

It's running your business with your voice, your heart, your integrity. Not for clicks, but for change.

It's walking away from toxic family dynamics, not with bitterness, but with boundaries and grace.

It's resting. Laughing. Loving. Waking up knowing you are safe in your own life.

It's legacy. It's freedom. It's peace.

It's being able to sit at your kitchen table with your loved ones, look around, and feel like you're finally home.

Prosperity, for me, is also legacy. I want my daughter and my bonus sons to know a world where boundaries are healthy, not harsh. Where healing is expected, not taboo. I want the women I coach to ripple this energy into their families, their communities, their future generations. I don't just coach, I plant seeds. And I believe the fruit we grow from those seeds will nourish more than just us.

To the woman still in the fire.

You are not too late.

You are not too broken.

You are not the problem.

You are the possibility.

Whatever your story has been, you have the power to write a new chapter. One with purpose. One with prosperity. One with peace.

Your life is not meant to be endured. It is meant to be lived: fully, freely, and fearlessly.

I am not telling this story because I made it out perfectly.

I'm telling it because I made it out powerfully.

And so will you.

Before you turn the page, I want you to ask yourself:

- What possibility have I been too afraid to believe in?
- What version of me is waiting to rise from the ashes?

Write it down. Speak it out loud.

Repeat this with me:
I am not too far gone.
I am not what they called me.
I am the author now.
I will no longer beg for room at tables I was meant to build.
I am the possibility.
And I rise, fully and fearlessly.

This story isn't just mine. It's yours, too. If you've lived through it, you can lead from it.

You are not here by accident. You are here because something inside you knows there's more: more to give, more to become, more to reclaim.

If you've ever felt invisible...
If you've ever shrunk yourself to make others more comfortable...
If you've been told you're too much, too loud, too emotional, too ambitious...

Let me be the one to tell you:

You are not too much.
You are a woman who has survived what others never even speak about.
You are a story of rising in human form.

I used to think my story disqualified me. That the trauma, the abuse, the silence made me "less than." But now I know better.

It made me ready.

There is power in being the one who breaks the cycle. The one who chooses healing over hatred. The one who says, "It ends with me."

And yes, it's hard. It's messy. It costs you relationships, illusions, and comfort. But it gives you back your soul.

And what could be more prosperous than finally feeling whole?

If you're standing at the edge of your next chapter, I want to offer you this:

You don't need to wait until you feel ready.
You don't need another certificate or title to be worthy.
You don't need permission from anyone.

All you need is the courage to say:
"This is not where my story ends."

The road from possibility to prosperity doesn't require perfection. It requires presence. And a decision to stop living on autopilot and start living on purpose.

So, don't dim yourself to fit into rooms that were never built for your light.
Build your own table. Speak your truth. Show others what's possible when a woman refuses to be silenced.

That's how we lead. That's how we rise.
That's how we transform pain into purpose.
That's how we turn survival into a movement.
That's how we go from possibility... to prosperity.

Your shift doesn't have to be loud. But it does have to be true.
You are the turning point someone else is waiting for.
You are the evidence that healing is real.
You are the proof that legacy begins in the heart of one brave woman who says:
"No more hiding. No more shrinking. I choose to rise."

Say it with me now:

I am not broken.
I am not behind.
I am not invisible.

I am the possibility.
And this is just the beginning.

Ariel Faith

Ariel Faith LLC
Visual Alignment Expert & Brand Photographer

https://www.linkedin.com/in/ariel-personalbranding
https://www.facebook.com/af.personalbranding
https://www.instagram.com/ariel.personalbranding/
https://arieljoyfaith.com
https://blog.arieljoyfaith.com

Ariel dances between what is and what could be. From dropout to drafting to Historic Design Consultant to transformational photographer and brand strategist, Ariel's unconventional journey bridges inner evolution and outer expression. What began as a tool during architectural work became her lifeline when photography emerged as therapy during COVID's stillness.

As a Gen X mom of 4 (3 Millennials and 1 Gen Z), Ariel built her business while homeschooling and making the conscious choice to put her children first, proving that heart-centered success doesn't require sacrificing what matters most.

Sometimes we lose everything, but it's the perfect place to start.

Ariel specializes in helping accomplished women whose souls have outgrown their photos, women whose wisdom deserves authentic expression.

Through her confidence in business courses, Brand Alignment Path cohorts, and commercial brand photography sessions, she guides women past perfectionism to authentic impact, integrating inner transformation with outer business success.

Host of the "You Matter in Business" podcast, Ariel, proves that powerful business transformations occur when visual presence aligns with inner evolution, where authentic authority emerges from transforming struggles into wisdom worth sharing.

I Was Poor Until I Learned to See

By Ariel Faith

When you learn to see beauty, you discover you're surrounded by treasure.

"Let's just try it. Who wants to come with me tonight?"

My photography instructor, Alan Shapiro, stood on a Chicago street corner at sunset, challenging our small group to do something that terrified me: photograph strangers. Real people. With real stories.

I was a nature photographer. Give me a landscape at golden hour, a macro shot of dewdrops on petals, or the soft abstraction of intentional camera movement, and I'm in my element. But people? People were complicated. Unpredictable. What if I couldn't capture them well? When you work with flowers, they dance in a field, not concerned about the flowers next to them or their wilted petals. They don't hide behind a mask of perfection. People—we are complicated.

Yet something in me, the growth-centered adventure seeker that occasionally overrode my practical, cautious side, whispered, "Why not?" The worst thing that could happen was getting some great shots of Chicago architecture at night.

I had no idea that decision would give me a new insight into what abundance looks and feels like.

The Small-Town Girl Meets the City

We walked from the Millionaire Mile district to the theater district that evening, from sunset to city lights. It had been a foggy week, giving an intense moodiness to the city, a photographer's dream, with secrets hidden in buildings behind dense clouds. But I wasn't thinking about architecture anymore.

As a small-town girl, city streets were not in my comfort zone, especially at night. Alan, seeing my lack of confidence in approaching strangers, decided to ease me in gently. "See that monk walking down the street?" he pointed. "Go ask if you can take his photo."

He looked harmless enough. I approached nervously, asked politely, and was kindly refused. Of course. Alan later told me he knew the monk would say no for religious reasons, but he wanted me to experience a rejection so I'd be willing to try again. Brilliant trick.

And it worked.

Three Women, Three Revelations

The first woman we encountered on that city walk was a street performer, a stunning, dark-skinned singer with a voice that filled the streets with rich, soulful tones. She agreed with apprehension, but as we began photographing, she lit up. What started as hesitation transformed into engagement as she sang her heart out, connecting not just with us but with everyone passing by.

Something stirred in me. This was different than photographing flowers.

Next, we met a Spanish woman with long, tight curls who was shooting her video in front of a tall sculpture of golden angel wings standing in a courtyard between two towering buildings. She was in the middle of filming herself live for her YouTube channel when we asked to photograph her. Magic happened. She told her audience, "This is a very special moment for me." She truly was angelic in her movement that night. I began to see this wasn't just about taking pictures. This was about connecting with the subject in the viewfinder.

But it was the third woman we met who deeply changed my vision that night.

The Dancer Who Taught Me About Being Seen

In a part of the city I would not normally find myself, we encountered a dancer and her crew trying to get people to join them at their club. She was stunning, but I could see something deeper. In the subtleties of her movements, in the way she carried herself, I saw a woman who was looked at but rarely truly seen. It was as if her outer beauty were a shield that protected her from being known.

When I asked if we could photograph her, something shifted. Under the streetlights, away from the club atmosphere, she began to shine. Not perform. Shine. There was a light in her eyes, a dignity in her posture, a beauty that had nothing to do with her external features and everything to do with being honored for who she was.

While I was watching her transform under my lens, while we talked and laughed between moments, my eyes were opened to something profound: the power of photography for people, especially women who are broken and afraid but willing to try. The power of being truly seen.

This wasn't just about taking pictures. This was about recognizing souls and seeing hearts.

The Success That Left Me Empty

To understand why that Chicago night was so transformational, you need to know where I'd come from professionally.

I had climbed to the top of my field in residential design. Starting as a drafter for architects and engineers, I eventually specialized in traditional homes with authentic details. This kind of craftsmanship was disappearing unless you were working on multi-million-dollar projects. I wanted to bring simple beauty back to the housing market, but I was fighting against an industry where "boxes are homes and windows are unwanted." Where money made design decisions, not the quality of light that windows allow into a space—building houses for cars rather than homes.

The pinnacle of my career was being asked to author two pattern books for the City of Lake Helen. One honored the existing historic homes and preserved the details that defined their architectural styles. The second was designed to help builders, architects, and designers understand these patterns and encourage new construction with design integrity. This work included documenting homes with my camera and creating visual guidelines for the historic district to maintain the quaint, timeless nature of this small, beautiful southern town. It was meaningful work, and I was called on as an expert in my field, which honestly felt good for a woman who dropped out of high school only to graduate ten years later. But this feeling was only brief.

It felt void. Completely void.

The impact was minimal at best. I could design beautiful spaces, but I wasn't personally touching lives. I wasn't connecting with souls. Success by traditional standards—titles, reputation, expertise, financial stability—left me feeling empty.

When Photography Became More Than Art

After the pattern book project, I dove into fine art photography as a hobby. I loved learning new techniques, new and old art lenses, intentional camera movement, abstraction, isolating small windows of larger scenes to focus on emotions, light, and dancing shapes. Impressionistic photography became my favorite. It was soft, subtle, and open to the viewers' emotions. It filled my heart for a time.

I worked with a few small galleries, sold a few fine art pieces, and explored macro work with flowers and nature. I traveled to beautiful places and found beauty in my backyard. I walked mountain trails seeking waterfalls and wildflowers and that pocket of light. I meandered on many a garden path. There is a gentle beauty in flowers, confirming what I knew long ago—that flowers were created to remind us of the delicacy and yet strong resilience that lives inside women.

Photography became my healthy way to deal with COVID-19 when normal life stopped. But in the end, this work was, too, just pretty pictures.

Until Chicago.

Until I realized that the same care I took to see the subtle differences in tulips, each one unique, each one carrying its own personality and energy, was exactly how I could begin to see people. I had never really noticed tulips before—they all looked the same. But as they age, something amazing happens: They break out of normalcy and begin to dance, full of individual character.

Learning to See Through Different Eyes

Then, a few months after the Chicago adventure, I began to shift my focus from portraits of flowers to portraits of women.

I had the honor to photograph a beautiful, tall Cuban woman named Barbara, a professional model I was working with in South Florida. She had long, dark brown hair and amber eyes. She had mastered the art of posing, how to hold her hands, how to position her body for maximum visual impact, and even the art of expression. Her poise was excellent and graceful. Her expressions were emotive to the viewer. Everything was technically perfect. Yet something was missing. She was posing for the camera, for me, the photographer, but not for herself. She was doing what she had learned to do well, but her soul wasn't connected to any of it. I could see it in the subtlety of her eyes.

After about fifteen minutes of this beautiful but empty perfection, I knew she was in there somewhere. I had seen her earlier that day when we were eating lunch, laughing about something, completely relaxed and radiant.

I set my camera down.

"Barbara," I said, "where do you feel most like yourself?"

She gazed out the window, and her whole demeanor softened. She told me about her hometown in Cuba, and as she spoke, her eyes softened. She shifted from posed to poised. A genuine smile replaced the rehearsed one as she described the music resonating through the streets and how she could still feel the rhythm in her heart. She talked about watching the children play with Coke cans and bottle caps as they raced them down the alley with such pride. She described how young and old would just dance in the streets, and this was normal. She explained how she lived among a community of family and friends, where every day was meant to be lived and enjoyed. As she spoke, I could hear the music with her and smell the Cuban food filling the streets at night.

She honored me with her genuine vulnerability. At first, she felt uncomfortable when I picked up my camera again. She did not know what to do when she was not performing. Sensing her discomfort, we began playing with some of the props in the room. A beautiful sequined long scarf became a safe place for her. She began to dance with it, hiding behind the transparent layers veiling her. She was enjoying the moment—that was the point. She shared her real moments with me and my lens. It was simple, playful, and her heart was open, her eyes real.

Later, she wrote in a review: "Ariel has a gift for creating a fun and creative atmosphere... The attention to detail and passion for the art are something you don't get with every photographer. Ariel has it!"

But what she gave me that afternoon was confirmation: Seeing and being seen is a gift. This was not just photography but seeing— seeing people. Really seeing them and helping them feel seen.

Before this realization, I didn't photograph people at all. I took pleasure in sharing the beauty of creation: flowers, landscapes, the subtle dance of light and shadow in nature. But this was different. This was about recognizing the profound impact these sessions could have on life transformation itself.

Now, even a year after a photo shoot, women tell me how much that session meant to them. They say they hated their photos until these—they never looked at themselves the same way again. They carry themselves differently. The business transformation was just the beginning; I began to see the life-changing impact these sessions could offer.

I do extensive preparation for all my sessions now: talking, getting to know the client, and listening. Often, the most impactful sentence is the one she doesn't say. When someone feels anxious, that's when you stop everything: put the camera down, learn and listen, give them permission to feel.

Because here's what I've learned: the strongest photographs come from the moments when someone feels safe enough to stop protecting themselves and start being themselves.

The Mask I Didn't Know I Was Wearing

Here's the thing about learning to see others clearly: You can't do it until you learn to see yourself.

For years, I wore a mask of "happy" so convincingly that I didn't even know my clinical depression wasn't happiness. My self-perception had become so distorted that I needed to find the me that was living inside, hidden.

Some call this your inner child. I like to think of it as your authentic self: the one that is honest and true, the one that loves and plays and enjoys seeing others shine. That woman has been there all along. She just wasn't safe.

Life is cruel to those who hide. It's almost like we wear a sign: "I have been abused, take your shot. I will stay silent in my fear." When I began seeing unhealthy coping skills being passed to my children, I knew I needed to dig deeper and find my value. I wasn't sure if it even existed, but I needed to try, for my children.

As a teenager, a friend once told me, "If you don't know who you are, find someone you want to be like and become that person." I remembered that conversation and used his wisdom as a first step on this unmasking and self-valuing journey that God carried me through.

The true breakthrough came when I learned and began to truly believe I have value in God's eyes, and nothing can change that. No matter what external situation I am in, or what lies someone says or chooses to believe.

What Honoring Your Worth Looks Like

Practically speaking, honoring your own worth is a peaceful awareness of your strengths and weaknesses. You honor your strengths, your natural talents and nurture them. You honestly see possibility and growth in your weaknesses. When you find a lie echoing in your head, you see it for what it is and quickly throw it in the garbage of your mind, where it belongs, and you make sure to take out the trash. You no longer need others to sing your praises or confirm your value for you.

This journey taught me to see myself in the way I was learning to see my photography subjects: not as broken things needing to be fixed, but as whole beings carrying stories worth honoring.

And once I could see myself that way, everything changed about how I saw first nature, flowers, and then people. I knew the value of taking the time to see.

When You See Your Value, You See Everything Differently

The breakthrough didn't stop with me. Once I learned to honor my own worth, it was like someone had given me new eyes.

Suddenly, I wasn't just seeing my photography subjects differently. I was seeing everyone differently. The cashier at the grocery store wasn't just someone scanning my items. She was someone with stories, dreams, and struggles I'd never know. The friend who always seemed perfect suddenly felt safe enough to share her real fears with me, because she sensed I was finally seeing myself clearly.

That's the beautiful ripple effect of valuing yourself: when you stop needing others to validate your worth, you become free to truly see theirs. When you're not desperately seeking recognition, you can offer recognition. When you're not performing for approval, you can create space for others to stop performing, too.

Every woman who sits across from me now gets the gift of being seen by someone who has learned to see herself. And here's what happens: They leave that session not just with beautiful photos, but with permission to see themselves and others through kinder eyes.

The joy multiplies. One person learning to see their value creates ripples that touch everyone around them.

Redefining True Abundance

Here's what I discovered: True fulfillment has never been about your bank account, your title, or your achievements.

True prosperity is about your value and vision.

It's seeing the sparkle in someone's eyes that others miss. It's noticing the twinkle in a drop of rain shining through the dappled light in the trees. It's recognizing the story in every gesture, every expression, every moment when someone drops their guard and lets you see who they really are. It's understanding that the woman sitting across from you, whether she's a professional model, a street performer, or someone who's never felt beautiful in her life, is a walking miracle. We are surrounded by beauty. We just have to open our eyes and look!

That's wealth that can't be stolen, diminished, or lost in a market crash.

That's being rich toward God.

The Invitation to See

Every time I meet or talk to a woman now, I patiently wait and listen and honor where she is in her journey. I watch for the sentence she doesn't say. I notice when her shoulders drop slightly and her breathing deepens. I see the moment when protection gives way to presence, when performance transforms into authenticity.

Because here's what that night walking along the streets in Chicago and every session since has taught me: We live in a world that's trained us to see scarcity. To notice what's missing, what's wrong, what needs to be fixed, filtered, or improved.

But when you learn to see with different eyes, when you start looking for beauty instead of flaws, for stories instead of perfection, for souls instead of surfaces, you realize you're surrounded by treasure.

Your Mirror Moment

So, here's my challenge to you: What if you started looking at your life through a different lens?

What if that woman in the grocery store checkout line isn't just someone slowing you down, but someone carrying stories you'll never know? What if your friend who always seems to have it together actually needs to be seen for who she really is underneath the performance?

What if the face looking back at you in the mirror, with all its imperfections and evidence of a life fully lived, is exactly the face you're supposed to have?

You are not invisible. You are not the exception to love. You are not too broken, too ordinary, too anything to matter. You are seen. You have always been seen.

And you are a magnificent treasure walking around in human form.

When you can see... You see real treasure. And once you start seeing, you'll never be poor again.

Tomeka Jones

Flawless Life Coaching
Life Coach

https://www.linkedin.com/in/tomeka-jones-1760322a8/
https://www.facebook.com/groups/flawlesslifecoaching
https://www.instagram.com/flawlesslifecoaching
www.flawlesslifecoaching.com

Tomeka Jones is a life coach, speaker, author, and founder of Flawless Life Coaching. A 23-year U.S. Air Force veteran and registered nurse, Tomeka is on a divine mission to help women heal, embrace their worth, and rise with confidence. Known for her resilience and radiant spirit, she empowers others through her signature FLAWS method and teaches how to shift from surviving to thriving. Tomeka is the author of Riding the Waves of Self Confidence and Cultivating the Inner Garden of Self-Love and Beauty, and co-author of multiple empowering anthologies, including Thank God It's Monday and Rising Through the Pain. Whether she's speaking on stage or coaching queens to live boldly, Tomeka leads with heart and purpose. When she's not pouring into women, she's spending time with her daughter, traveling, or rocking one of her signature statement tees. Her journey proves that with faith and mindset, prosperity is possible.

Becoming HER: Possibility to Prosperity

By Tomeka Jones

As a Logistics Technician in the United States Air Force, precision wasn't optional—it was survival. I can still see myself driving the forklift through the PartStore warehouse, sweat dripping as I hauled pallets stacked with boxes of aircraft parts—heat rising off the concrete floor so thick you could've fried an egg on the floor. Fast forward a few years, and there I was as a Personnelist, buried under stacks of paperwork so tall they could qualify as cardio. And let's not forget my chapter as a nurse, juggling IV poles, vital signs, and patients who wanted to tell me their entire life story at 3 a.m. The roles were different, but the rhythm was the same: serve, sacrifice, repeat. Somewhere between the uniform, the checklists, and the stethoscopes, I wondered, *Who am I when the mission ends?*

No matter the job, the lesson was the same: you show up when your body aches and your soul is tired. You give without applause. You fight silent battles and carry invisible scars. And through it all, you learn that true excellence isn't about being seen—it's about the unseen sacrifices that keep the mission, and the people, alive.

But what nobody prepares you for is this: When the uniform comes off... so does a part of your identity. And that's where the real mission begins.

This book is for women leaving service-driven careers—those who have spent years giving everything to duty, only to step into civilian life feeling like their identity, confidence, and clarity got left behind. You will walk away with the courage to reclaim your voice, the tools to rebuild your purpose, and the blueprint to create prosperity on your own terms. Through raw storytelling, humor-laced truths, and practical frameworks like *The Flawless Five*, which we will discuss later on in the chapter. This chapter in the book doesn't just inspire—it equips you to rise again, grounded in who you are beyond the role you once played.

The Unwritten Orders After Retirement

When I retired from the United States Air Force in October 2022, I walked away with accolades, a shiny rank, and a resume full of accomplishments. But I also walked away with a quiet, lingering ache, a void I couldn't name. In the months that followed, 2023, in particular, I found myself waking up without reveille, without a mission briefing, early morning huddles, without the structure that had dictated my days for 23 years. The silence of civilian mornings was deafening. My calendar wasn't full of Commander Calls or training exercises; it was blank, and that blankness whispered, *"Now what?"*

One evening, as I sat at the kitchen table staring at my untouched journal, my daughter looked up at me and asked, *"Mom, why do you look so sad when you're supposed to be happy you retired?"* I paused, searching for words, but all I could manage was a weak smile and a soft, *"I don't know, baby. I thought this would feel different."*

That simple exchange externalized what I had been carrying inside the ache of purpose unanchored. The ribbons and awards sat neatly framed on the wall, but they could not tell me who I was outside the uniform. The Air Force had trained me to lead, to endure, to serve but not how to start over when the orders stopped coming. I served with pride. Supported global missions. Checked every box society had handed me. I was grateful, but something was missing. I wasn't just stepping out of a career, I was stepping into the unknown. And deep inside, I knew I wasn't done yet. There was a voice small at first, but steady that whispered, *"You were made for more."* It wasn't about chasing status or success. It was about alignment. It was about impact. It was about **becoming HER** the woman I was always meant to be, beyond the battlefield. That whisper? That was my purpose, trying to get my attention.

A New Kind of Calling

At first, I tried to ignore it. I stayed busy. I wore the title of "veteran" and "mom" like armor. I volunteered. I helped everyone else. I tried to keep living by the old rules in a new world.

But the whisper grew louder. It echoed in conversations with women who were stuck, broken, or settling. It stirred during late-night reflections. It tugged at me every time I spoke life into someone else even when I was secretly feeling lost myself.

One evening in **2023**, after another long day of self reflecting, I walked past the bathroom mirror on my way to bed. The apartment was quiet, my daughter was in school and I caught a glimpse of myself in the dim light. For a moment, I didn't see the uniform, the ribbons, or the titles. I saw a woman carrying both strength and exhaustion. And it hit me. The trigger wasn't the silence, it was the recognition that every word I had been speaking into other women was the very word I needed to speak into myself. I leaned on the counter, staring at my own reflection, and a thought rose from deep within: *"You've led in the military. Now it's time to lead in a new way— from the inside out."*

And just like that in **2024**, Flawless Life Coaching was born—not from perfection, but from purpose. From pain. From potential. From power.

From the Battlefield to Becoming HER

Let me keep it all the way real: I didn't step into business with a perfect plan. I didn't have a strategy, a brand, or even a clue where to start. What I did have was a deep desire to help women especially mothers, military sisters, healthcare workers, and entrepreneurs rediscover their confidence and rebuild their lives with clarity and courage.

I had lived the trauma. Faced the fear. Fought the imposter syndrome. Wrestled with doubt. And I had done it all while wearing a smile and raising a child. Military life had trained me to push through. To stay silent. To lead with grit, not vulnerability.

But stepping into my calling? That required a whole new level of bravery. I had to peel off the armor. I had to speak my truth. I had to stop hiding behind service and step into my soul work. And let me tell you, it wasn't easy.

Some months, I stared at my bank account wondering how I would cover business expenses while keeping the lights on at home. The decision to invest in a coach, build a website, or even print materials meant sacrificing things I once considered non-negotiable. On top of that, time never seemed to be on my side. Between a full-time job, raising my daughter, and managing life after the military, the only hours left to work on my dream were late at night when exhaustion whispered, *"just quit."*

But I refused. I showed up tired. I showed up scared. I showed up broke some days but I still showed up. Because prosperity doesn't start with perfect conditions; it starts with the courage to keep building, even when the resources are scarce and the clock is working against you. That's where the real prosperity begins.

The Whisper in YOU

If you're reading this right now and something in your spirit is stirring—listen. That business you can't stop thinking about? That book idea scribbled in your journal? That dream that feels too big, too bold, or too far away? That's not random. That's the purpose. That's possibility. And it's whispering to you—just like it whispered to me.

You don't have to have it all figured out. You don't need a website, a logo, or even a business card. What you need is to believe. Because HER—the future version of you who's healed, whole, confident, and wildly successful—she's already inside of you. Waiting.

The Teachers Who Helped Me Become HER

No one becomes HER alone. Behind every empowered woman is a lineage of wisdom—mentors, coaches, authors, voices that speak directly to your soul and invite you to rise. I've had many pivotal voices in my journey, but three have transformed not just how I lead, but how I live.

Each one, in their unique way, handed me keys to unlock the next level of my purpose. And because I'm all about turning pain into power and purpose into prosperity, I now use those keys to unlock doors for the women I coach. Let's talk about how their insights shaped my becoming—and how they can shape yours.

Nisa Nichols: The Power of Owning All of You

When I first encountered Nisa Nichols' work, I was already deep in my transition—from the uniform to the boardroom, from the battlefield to the business world. But something about the way she teaches identity work lit a fire in me. I resonated, and I could identify with her story.

Lisa doesn't just teach you to build a brand—she teaches you to **own your confidence**. To own your story. To own your scars. To own your superpowers. She helped me see that it wasn't just my credentials or my military history that made me qualified—it was my lived experience. The heartbreak. The breakdowns. The rebuilding. That's the foundation of my magic.

From Nisa, I learned how to show up boldly as the **whole** woman I am—not just the polished version, not just the accolades, but the messy, real, powerful parts too. Because that's what connects. Now, I teach my clients the same. I tell them: Your story is not a setback. It's a setup for your success! You don't have to hide your past. You get to package it. Position it. And profit from it—not in a manipulative way, but in a mission-driven way. Your authenticity is your currency.

Bob Proctor: The Mindset Blueprint for Prosperity

And then came Bob Proctor. The first time I heard him say, *"You were born rich,"* I felt something snap into place. Not because I had a bank full of money at the time (I didn't), but because he was speaking about identity. Energy. Belief. He taught me that prosperity is an inside job. Bob Proctor made me understand the difference between wishing and expecting. He said:

"You don't get what you want. You get what you are."

And whew—that hit me hard. Because I realized that all the vision boards, all the journals, all the declarations meant nothing if I didn't start embodying HER. So, I began doing the work. I studied how my subconscious mind was running the show. I practiced visualization daily—seeing HER in full detail. I reprogrammed the beliefs I had inherited:

– You have to work twice as hard.
– Money is hard to come by.
– It's selfish to want more.

Lies.

I replaced them with truths like:

✔ I am worthy now.
✔ Money comes to me with ease and purpose.
✔ My desires are divine.

Now, I pass those teachings on to my clients. I help them shift their paradigms—because without that inner shift, the outer success never sticks. When you shift your belief system, you shift your bank account. You shift your relationships. You shift your results. That's what Bob gave me-the blueprint to become HER by design—not by default.

Mel Robbin's "Let Them"

Then came one of the simplest, most liberating teachings I've ever heard—Mel Robbins' "Let Them." She said, "If they don't support you? Let them. If they don't invite you? Let them. If they don't understand your dream? Let them." At first, I didn't get it. I was still deep in my people-pleasing, approval-chasing era. I wanted everyone to clap for me, validate me, and believe in me. But HER? HER doesn't need permission. HER doesn't chase acceptance. HER doesn't beg for people to stay.

So, I stopped trying to force people to support a vision they couldn't see. I started releasing with grace. Let them misunderstand you. Let them doubt you. Let them walk away. It's not rejection. It's redirection. Now, *"Let Them"* is a mantra I repeat often. I pass it to my clients like a holy offering. It's freedom in two words. And let me tell you something: The moment you let them, you make space for the women, the mentors, the clients, the connections who are aligned with your next level. Letting go is an act of leadership. Of faith. Of trust. You don't need everyone to get it. You just need to keep moving.

HER Lives in You Right Now

So many women think they'll become HER after they hit a milestone—after they lose the weight, land the clients, hit six figures, find the partner, or grow their following. But that's backwards. HER shows up *before* the results. HER shows up in the **choice**. In the **habits**.

In the way you carry yourself, even when no one's watching.

Becoming HER is about:

Thinking differently
Speaking with certainty
Moving with intention
Showing up with purpose

You don't have to earn HER. You just have to **activate her**.

The Moment That Changed Everything: Mindset Over Mission

One of the most radical truths I had to accept was this: You don't build a business from strategy alone. You build it from identity.

Strategy is the plan—the marketing funnels, the pricing models, the business cards, the launch dates. Strategy tells you what to do and when to do it. It's important, but it's not the foundation.

Identity, on the other hand, is the core of who you are and what you believe about yourself. Identity answers the deeper questions: Do I see myself as worthy of success? Do I believe I have something valuable to offer? Am I willing to show up fully as me, even when fear whispers that I'm not enough?

Strategy might help you start, but identity is what makes you stay. Without identity, you'll sabotage the strategy. Without a clear sense of who you are, every setback feels like a stop sign instead of a stepping stone. But when your identity is rooted in truth—when you know who you are and whose you are—you can weather failure, rejection, and doubt because you're no longer building on shaky ground.

That was the moment everything shifted for me: when I stopped obsessing over the perfect strategy and started aligning with my authentic identity. That's when my mission came alive.

In the military, we were trained to obey, to push through, to do what had to be done. But in entrepreneurship, that hustle energy can only take you so far. To thrive, you must shift from grind mode to growth mode. From *"What if I fail?"* to *"What if I fly?"* From *"I don't know how,"* to *"I'll figure it out."* From *"I'm not enough,"* to *"I was born for this."* And that shift? It unlocks everything. Because we don't attract what we wish for—we attract what we embody.

Becoming HER Isn't Just a Journey. It's a Decision.

HER is not some distant version of you in the future. She's the woman you choose to be right now. She walks with certainty. Speaks with conviction. Loves herself boldly. Charges what she's worth. Shows up—even when it's messy, scary, or inconvenient. She doesn't ask for permission. She takes up space. She doesn't shrink. She expands. She's not waiting for perfect timing—she's building it. Becoming HER means taking radical ownership of your identity, your energy, and your destiny.

Let's get even more practical. Want to know how I keep becoming HER—on days when it's hard, when I'm tired, when imposter syndrome sneaks in? I use this exact powerful practice-**Becoming HER tool-kit**—and I give it to my clients too. This is a very strong toolkit. It consist of 5 minutes of visioning, 60-sec affirmations, 1 aligned goal, and 3-minutes of gratitude and release.

MORNING VISIONING (5 minutes)

I start every day by visualizing HER.

– How she walks.
– What she's celebrating.
– How her clients are thriving.
– How she feels when she checks her bank account.

I see her so clearly that I feel like I'm already her. Because I am.

POWER AFFIRMATIONS (60 Seconds)

I speak words that shape my reality.
"I am magnetic."
"My value is non-negotiable."
"I attract aligned opportunities with ease."
"I am HER—here and now."

ALIGNED ACTION (One action)

Every day, I do one thing that brings HER closer.
– Sending the email.
– Going live.
– Pitching the brand.
– Posting the offer.
– Saying no to something that drains me.

One step every day keeps the dream in motion.

EVENING GRATITUDE & RELEASE (3 minutes)

At night, I thank HER.
I celebrate progress, not perfection.
And I release any fear, doubt, or shame that crept in.

Becoming HER isn't a destination. It's a daily decision.

Redefining Prosperity—On Your Terms

Let's talk about the *prosperity* for a second. Most people think it's just about money. But true prosperity is deeper than that. Prosperity is waking up without anxiety. It's building a business that reflects your soul. It's laughing with your kids and not worrying about bills. It's walking into a room knowing you belong. It's knowing your worth— even if no one claps. And yes, it's also income, influence, and impact. But money follows the mission. Abundance follows alignment. You want an overflow? Start within.

There was a time I believed I had to choose between success and peace. Between being present for my daughter and building the life I envisioned. Between being strong for everyone else and finally choosing *me*. But I've learned—*you don't have to choose*. You are worthy of it all. Fulfillment, freedom, financial abundance, deep love, aligned purpose, impact, and joy. Not one or the other. All of it.

Too many people are out here performing success—smiling on the outside while silently unraveling something or struggling on the inside. Living for the applause but starving for authenticity? That's not prosperity. That's survival dressed up in designer labels and highlight reels. Real prosperity is soul-deep. It's walking in rooms without shrinking. It's resting without guilt. It's no longer begging to be seen, heard, or valued—because you already *know* who you are.

Prosperity is about rewriting the rules. This is about becoming so aligned, so anchored, so unapologetically grounded in your truth that abundance has no choice but to follow. That kind of life doesn't come from hustling harder—it comes from healing deeper. It comes from choosing to *believe*, even when the evidence isn't clear yet. That's when true prosperity shows up—not just in your bank account, but in your peace, your purpose, and your power.

You are the evidence. You are the legacy. You are the definition of prosperity—on your terms.

The Flawless Five: From Possibility to Profit

So, where do you begin? You don't need to burn it all down or launch an empire overnight. You just need five bold, beautiful steps. I call them **The Flawless Five**—the same blueprint that helped me turn purpose into profit.

Case Study: Meet Jasmine

Jasmine, a 34-year-old nurse and single mom, felt stuck in the cycle of "just enough." She wanted to launch a coaching business to help other women in healthcare manage stress and burnout, but fear and overwhelm held her back. By walking through The Flawless Five, Jasmine shifted from doubt to determination—and within months, she turned her idea into income.

Step 1: Write the Vision, Speak the Truth

Take the lid off your dreams. Don't write what's practical. Write what's powerful.

What would life look like if you stopped playing small?

What would your bank account, schedule, and relationships reflect if you fully owned your brilliance?

Write it. And then speak it. Every. Single. Day.

Your words have power. Speak possibility, not fear.

- **Objective:** Anchor your success in clarity and confession—what you write and speak shapes what you create.
- **10-Minute Task:** Journal a "no-limits" vision of your dream life—career, money, health, and relationships.
- **24-Hour Challenge:** Record yourself reading your vision aloud and listen back before bed.
- **7-Day Win Metric:** Speak your vision out loud daily; track shifts in confidence or mindset in your journal.
- **Case Study:** Jasmine wrote her dream of leaving 12-hour shifts behind and building a coaching practice that gave her both freedom and financial stability. Speaking it daily made it feel less like a fantasy and more like a plan.

Step 2: Serve Before You Sell

Don't wait for the perfect funnel or fancy brand kit. Start now. Start messy.

Coach for free. Go live on social. Share your journey. Teach what you know.

Clarity comes through movement—not perfection.

You don't need to prove your worth with prices. You need to prove your impact through service.

- **Objective:** Build credibility and confidence through action, not polish.
- **10-Minute Task:** Write a short post sharing one lesson from your own journey and post it on social media.
- **24-Hour Challenge:** Offer a free 20-minute coaching call to one person in your network.
- **7-Day Win Metric:** Serve at least 3 people (free call, post, or live session) and note feedback.
- **Case Study:** Jasmine went live on Facebook about how she overcame burnout. Three colleagues reached out immediately, thanking her for sharing—and one asked if she would mentor them.

Step 3: Treat Your Purpose Like a Mission

Remember how seriously you took deployment? How committed you were once?

That's how seriously you should treat your dream.

Set deadlines. Create structure. Build systems. Make a plan—and stick to it.

Your purpose isn't a hobby. It's your legacy.

- **Objective:** Shift your mindset from casual effort to disciplined execution.
- **10-Minute Task:** Block out one hour on your calendar this week exclusively for your business.
- **24-Hour Challenge:** Write down 3 non-negotiables you'll commit to in building your dream.
- **7-Day Win Metric:** Track completion of at least 70% of the tasks you commit to this week.

- **Case Study:** Jasmine treated her coaching dream like she treated her nursing shifts—non-negotiable. She blocked out evenings after her son's bedtime for business-building instead of scrolling social media.

Step 4: Elevate Your Environment

You can't become HER in the same rooms where you were doubted, dismissed, or drained.

Get in spaces that stretch you. Invest in mentorship. Attend live events. Join masterminds. Hire the coach.

You need people who remind you of your power when you forget.

- **Objective:** Surround yourself with environments and people that reflect where you're going, not where you've been.
- **10-Minute Task:** Identify one mentor, group, or community that inspires you and follow/connect today.
- **24-Hour Challenge:** Remove one draining influence— unfollow a negative social account, or say no to an energy-draining obligation.
- **7-Day Win Metric:** Engage with a growth environment (group, mentor, event, or accountability partner) at least twice this week.
- **Case Study:** Jasmine joined a local women's business mastermind. Hearing other women share their challenges and wins gave her courage to speak about her own vision— and reminded her she wasn't alone.

Step 5: Embody HER Now

Who is the version of you that already has what you want?

How does she move?

What does she believe?

What habits does she keep?

What boundaries does she hold?

Start acting like HER today.

- **Objective:** Align your present actions with the identity of your future self.
- **10-Minute Task:** Write down three habits your "HER" already lives by—and start practicing one today.
- **24-Hour Challenge:** Dress, walk, or speak as if you are already the successful version of yourself.
- **7-Day Win Metric:** Practice at least one "HER habit" every day for a week and note changes in confidence.
- **Case Study:** Jasmine began showing up on Zoom calls as if she already had a roster of clients—professional background, confident tone, clear boundaries. Soon, women began treating her like the coach she had envisioned herself to be.

Start acting like **HER** today.

Identity creates reality. The more you embody HER, the faster she manifests.

The Truth Most People Won't Tell You

This journey isn't easy. It's not always affirmations and wins. There were nights I cried on my bathroom floor. Mornings, I wanted to give up. Moments, I questioned everything. But every single time, I remembered: I'm not just building a business. I'm building a legacy. I'm building a model for my daughter. I'm becoming the woman I needed growing up. And that makes it all worth it. There were times I showed up to coach others with a smile while silently battling my storm. Times I gave everything I had to pour into someone else's healing while praying to God for the strength to hold mine together. But purpose has a way of pulling us forward even when pain tries to hold us back. I realized I wasn't just showing up for me I was showing up for every woman who's ever felt unseen, unheard, and unworthy.

Every hard day, every setback, every tear has become part of my testimony. The days when my uniform was soaked with sweat and my heart was heavy with doubt, the nights I cried quietly in the dark so no one could see my breaking point, the moments I felt invisible even while carrying the weight of responsibility all of it has been woven into my story. Those struggles weren't wasted; they became the bricks that built my resilience, the fire that refined my character, and the soil where the seeds of my prosperity were planted. What once felt like obstacles are now the very chapters that prove possibility is real.

This Chapter Is For YOU, Sis

You've given to everyone else for years. You've worn the uniform. Played the role. Kept the peace. Carried the weight. Stayed silent. But now is **Your Time**. Time to say yes to you. Time to build a life and business that turns heads and changes lives. Time to walk boldly into your next chapter—unapologetically. And sis, if you're in that valley right now—know this: Your pain is valid, but it will not be wasted. HER isn't just a vibe. She's a decision. She's a declaration. And she's your divine assignment.

You've waited long enough, sis. This chapter is your permission slip to stop dimming your light and start designing a life that reflects your power, purpose, and potential. It's time to trade in survival mode for overflow. The vision God placed in your heart wasn't random—it's your roadmap. Your dreams didn't come to tease you. They came to *teach* you what's possible. So, show up. Speak up. And level up. Your destiny is calling, and HER is ready.

Your Prosperity Is Inevitable

Prosperity isn't a far-off dream—it's a decision you affirm daily through your habits, thoughts, and actions. To help you build momentum, here's a **7-Day Starter Plan** you can use right now. Small, consistent steps create unstoppable results.

☑ **Day 1 – Write It Down**
Take 10 minutes to journal your vision of a prosperous life—what it looks like in your finances, relationships, and health.

☑ **Day 2 – Speak It Out**
Say your vision out loud in the mirror. End your sentence with: *"My prosperity is inevitable."*

☑ **Day 3 – Clear One Block**
Remove one distraction, debt, or draining task from your week that steals your energy.

☑ **Day 4 – Serve Someone**
Give value without expecting anything in return—encourage, mentor, or share a resource.

☑ **Day 5 – Invest in You**
Spend at least 30 minutes learning, reading, or practicing something that grows your mindset or skills.

☑ **Day 6 – Align Your Space**
Declutter one area of your home, office, or digital world. Prosperity flows in order, not chaos.

☑ **Day 7 – Celebrate Progress**
Write down 3 wins from this week—big or small. Then thank God (and yourself) for the steps you've taken.

Let me remind you of something sacred:

You are **not too late**.
      You are **not too old**.
      You are **not too much**.
      You are **right on time**.

The whisper in your spirit is divine. It's real. It's holy. And it's waiting for you to stop doubting and start doing. Prosperity isn't just about building a business—it's about reclaiming your power. Because when a woman chooses herself, chooses healing, and chooses abundance—HER whole world shifts.

So go ahead...

Write your vision.
Speak your truth.
Show up boldly.
Charge what you're worth.
Take the leap.

You've worn boots. You've fought battles. You've carried burdens. Now it's time to wear your crown. NOW is the time to become HER.

My Challenge to You

- Grab a journal and write down your vision—no limits, no edits.
- Speak one affirmation about HER every morning.
- Take one bold step toward your business this week.
- Join a room, community, or program that expands you.
- And most importantly... *trust yourself*.

Your future is flawless. And *prosperity* is already yours. Let's Go!

-BecomingHer
Tomeka Jones
www.flawlesslifecoaching.com

FB Page: https://www.facebook.com/FlawlessLifeCoaching (@FlawlessLifeCoaching)

Fb Group: https://www.facebook.com/groups/flawlesslifecoaching (@flawlesslifecoaching)

Instagram: https://www.instagram.com/flawlesslifecoaching/ (@flawlesslifecoaching)

LinkedIn: https://www.linkedin.com/in/flawlesslifecoaching/ (@flawlesslifecoaching)

Linktree: https://linktr.ee/flawlesslife

Youtube: https://www.youtube.com/@flawlesslifecoaching (@flawlesslifecoaching)

Anna Barboza Lugo

Pure Tea Love
Business Owner of Pure CBD Love, Pure Tea Love & Pure Love
Travel, Entrepreneur, Mentor, Mother, And Child of God

https://www.linkedin.com/in/anna-lugo-62746219/
https://www.facebook.com/@women.inspiring.women.2024
https://www.instagram.com/Alohalugo/
https://www.instagram.com/Up2uGod
https://www.puretealove.com/
https://www.women-inspiring-women-and-men-too.com
http://www.travoruim.com/purelovetravel.com

Anna Barboza Lugo is a retired information technology professional, a single mother, a mentor, a sister, and most importantly a Child of God. She is the proud owner of Pure CBD Love, Pure Tea Love and Pure Love Travel. She is a five time best selling author and soon to be a 6th time best selling author with the release of this masterpiece. She is a new Bestselling Author of a Book Guide to Living Your Best Life. Anna used to host her own Tea'V show called "We have a Tea for That... Positivi-Tea!" Her motto in life is "I'm Too Blessed To Be Stressed" because everything is Up2uGod." Her Chapter is called "Spirituali-Tea' is my Priori-Tea' for Eterni-Tea!.. She always created and organically grew a social media page called "UP2UGOD" that reached 2.7 million souls.

From Scarci-Tea' to Prosperi-Tea' to Generosi-Tea!

By Anna Barboza Lugo

WE HAVE A TEA FOR THAT... PROSPERI-TEA!!

You will often hear me say, "We Have A 'Tea' For That." It's a slogan I created for my Tea Business, Pure Tea Love.

Hello my name is Anna Barboza Lugo and I am the proud owner of Pure Tea Love and Pure CBD Love. I am a retired IT professional, a single mother, an Author, and a child of God. I am a humbled, confident, independent, passionate, loving, leader and God fearing woman.

Yes, we do have a Tea for that...This is a story of how I went from Scarci-Tea' to Prosperi-Tea', to Generosi-Tea!!

In my first anthology book called *Guide to Living your Best Life*, I had a similar title called Spirituali-Tea' is my Priori-Tea', for Eterni-Tea', because I put God first in everything I do, including my finances.

Did you know that God wants us to be rich? It's true, He only wants the first ten percent.

Well let's define Rich. Rich does not always mean money. I used to think "rich" meant you had to have a lot of money or come from a family of wealth. Today, my definition of richness means peace with God, and love for others and being a blessing. It's leaving a legacy of Integri-Tea' behind, and wise stewardship of whatever He places in my hands. What even more truer is that our Wealth is our Health. My sister's father-in-law, Rudy, would always tell me, you're rich Anna! And I would always reply that I am Rich In Blessings. It's true, I have things in life that money can't buy, and I've acquired many of those. But the best things are those you can't put a price tag on. Things like happiness, joy, peace, love, forgiveness, and I can go on and on.

Let me tell you how God led me from Scarci-Tea' and Pover-Tea', to living with Possibili-Tea' and Prosperi-Tea', and how I turned it into being a Genorosi-Tea' Rockstar at our local church which is a blessing and Priori-Tea' in my life. Giving makes me just as happy as the ones who are blessed to receive. I am beyond grateful that God uses my pockets to bless my local church communi-tea's, as well as many other chari-tea's near and dear to my heart. Giving makes a huge impact in our world. Being purpose driven as a single mother myself, I often support Single Mother organizations such as Embrace Grace. Its a movement with chapters being formed in churches to help single pregnant moms choose pro life and pro love. Gracefully Living is another organization that helps build homes for pregnant mothers. We were blessed to build and construct a teen pregnant center at St. Judes Ranch in Las vegas along side my leadership Tea'm. My daughter and I have made it a tradition to adopt single mothers at Christmas time and love to make a positive impact on women who've been in my shoes.

Now that I'm retired, I choose to live a life of Simplici-Tea', Sereni-Tea' and Tranquili-Tea'. It's truly a blessing to reach my financial goals that I set out to achieve this year. When you set clear financial goals and let God orchestrate the moves, it's such an exhilarating feeling when it finally happens. All Glory to God for answered prayers. I've prayed for this and its finally happening. To be debt free is a fantastic feeling. To achieve financial Securi-tea' has been a key goal since I became a mom.

I believe God blesses us so we can be a blessing to others. He has blessed my pockets so I can pay it forward. He has rooted me to be in service with faith, passion and Digi-tea'. I will always give "Thanks" to the Lord for providing our every need. I even had a license plate called Thx2God & Up2uGod. Because I am so Thankful Everything is

Up to Him. His timing is always perfect and He's never a minute late, but always right on time. I will never forget the days when we lived in Harbor City; It was Christmas 1968, and we heard a knock at the door. It was the local church who brought us boxes of food from a local Chari–tea'. They left us a Christmas tree with five wrapped gifts. Three girls, one boy and one for our mom. This left a lasting impression on me so much that I will never forget that pivotal moment when I knew I wanted to be the hands and feet of the "Givers". This would be my sole purpose in life. I will never forget my humbling beginnings, especially during our time of need. I love that I can come from a place of Humili-Tea' with Digni-Tea' and Vulnerabili-tea'.

I believe God wants us to be rich in health and in wealth, rich in blessings, rich in love, rich in Generosi-Tea', and rich with Prosperi-Tea, and of course, rich with Plen-Tea' of Opportuni-Tea's. People often think that being rich is related to money and it most certainly can be, I, on the other hand, look at money as a tool to become financially secure and free from debt. It's been a long term goal I set in motion years ago to create a life toward financial freedom.

Well this past year I set a goal to pay off my home I've owned for 28 years and become debt free from house mortgages to car notes to credit cards. I have successfully achieved that goal and recently experienced Christmas in July of 2025. I'm excited to enter a new chapter with new beginnings in Daytona Beach, Florida. I know how blessed I am because the good Lord has blessed be with enough cash to purchased a convertible BMW and lease a condo in Daytona Beach shores on the beach and give generously to our church and other important chari-tea's. It's always been a dream of mine to live on a beach. And to do it debt free is truly a dream come true…. All Glory belongs to Almighty God. How did I do it… It was Mindset… I set my heart and mind with clear intention. Many years ago I learned a habit to Dream', Declare' and Deliver. I'll go into that a little bit more later.

It is by investing and managing what God blessed me with. Afterall, He does ask us to multiply and grow and expand. He also asks us to trust and give and tithe. He trusts us to be obedient and navigate and invest in the little He gave us to make it much more. It can become difficult when you're in an unfamiliar territory and haven't learned how to spend carefully and save wisely. I had to learn how to think and grow rich in the eyes of the Lord.

To become a financially independent woman has always been my ultimate goal. It has been a goal since 1979' when I became a single mother at 7 months pregnant, with no insurance. I had to learn how to show up not just for me, but for my daughter too. We didn't have a lot of money as i entered motherhood, and most of my money went to pay for having my child. I learned at a very young age what it meant to "Just Get By". When I say Just Get By: it was definitely a real struggle living off of social security month after month, paycheck to paycheck. We lived in Pover-Tea' before I even understood what poverty was. By the end of the month we were dead broke. But we always had rice and beans and homemade tortillas and of course we had each other. I didn't come from a home with privileges or wealth or an inheritance. Before daddy passed, we had the best of everything. My sister told me my daddy was a hard worker who made sure we had the best clothes on our backs and plenty of food on our tables. Then after daddy passed, my mother struggled and moved us from Texas to Redondo Beach and Hermosa Beach with her family briefly before landing in the projects of Harbor City in 1968. We lived there until mom met our Papa Georgie (our step dad) and he moved us out of the projects into a beautiful home in Redondo Beach in late 1969 early 1070's. I remember going to a new school with new friends, new clothes and we even had a helmsman truck drive by selling milk and huge cream puffs. Life changed for the better.

My mom did the best she could, being a widowed single mother of four l children. Back then, we were not rich in terms of wealth, but we had each other, and if you were not rich during that time, it was as if we were being shamed, bullied or judged for not having money or budget to do things. I know now that we needed to have a budget, but, how can you do that when there was no money left over to budget? I watched my mom struggle month after month. I guess that made me want to provide even more to my child once I became a mom. To achieve financial Securi-Tea has always been my ultimate goal.

To be able to come from a place of barely enough to more than enough is truly a blessing. To grow from a limited belief of Scarci-Tea' to Prosperi-Tea' has truly been hard work and required a lot of focus and sacrifices, a lot of soul searching, a lot of break-throughs. It's always been my goal and dream to become financially independent and debt free. My goal this year was to eliminate all my debt so that I can really enjoy my retirement without the worry if I would make money in my businesses to stay afloat. I said to myself, this year I am done struggling financially. It's time to make some big moves and boy did I.

God says in his word that He promises to give us a hope and a future and supply all our needs. I believe in His word and His work

I live by Jeremiah 29:11

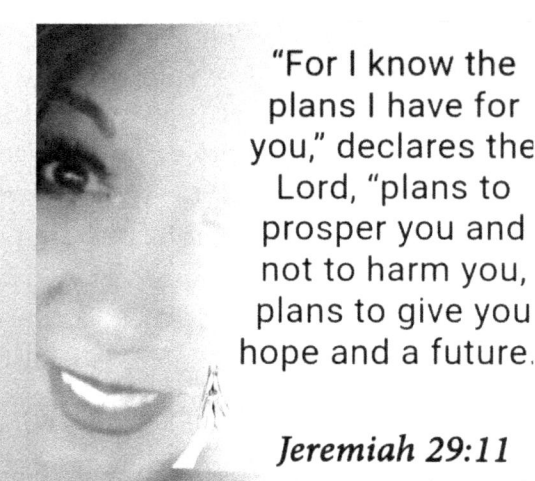

"For I know the plans I have for you," declares the Lord, "plans to prosper you and not to harm you, plans to give you hope and a future.

Jeremiah 29:11

For I know the plans I have for you, declares the Lord, plans to prosper you and not harm you, plans for a future and hope.

I live off of this principle. It was even the code to my alarm for my previous home.

It has not been an easy journey to get to a point in life where you feel financially independent and free. It took a lot of hard work, a lot of twists and turns, a lot of sacrifices, a lot of ups and downs, and definitely a lot of lessons, failures and most importantly successes. There were no handouts or inheritance to rely on, only my hard work and my Father in heaven watching over me. Abba Father and Thank you, Daddy!

I also learned that you can have all the money in the world and still be miserable. Money can not buy love or happiness. Happiness must come from within. Money also can't buy peace, sleep, mercy, or Gods gentle graces.

We have a choice to wake up everyday. I learned that life is about choices. I went through a leadership course where I learned that we have a choice for everything in life. We can choose happiness over sadness, and we can be hopeful that each day is a fresh new beginning. We get to choose to be positive in a negative world. We get to choose our goals, our paths to greatness, our habits, our boundaries, and our relationships. I always say "If the Ships in life are not taking you places, it is best to abandon ship. Partnerships, Relationships, Friendships, Companionship, Mentorships, Fellowship, Entrepreneurship are important to the backbone to your successes. Let that sink in... See Everything in life is a Choice YOU get to choose.

Let's do an exercise to get our Creativi-Tea' juices flowing as we pour into some new habits. Lets create a habit whereby you develop a list of three tasks you will complete each day.

This will be called a "Dream, Declare, Deliver" task that must be done consecutively for 100 days. After 100 days this will become a habit that you've developed.

Let's break it down from a birdeyes view as we brew up some Positivi-tea and pour out some important tips as we sip these tea's, one task at a Time...

Accountabili-Tea':

Have an accountability partner, mentor, coach or someone who can hold your feet to the fire. Are you taking action or just speaking words?

Schedule a time between 8:00am and 9:00am each morning to dream, declare and deliver three things you will accomplish for the day.

Example:

Day 1 Tasks - Today l will accomplish these three tasks by 9:00pm

1. Be a blessing to others and hand out lunch bags to the homeless from the brown bag ministry
2. Transfer money between checking and savings
3. Take my daughter to dinner

Day 2 Task - Today I will complete these three tasks by 9:00pm

1. Schedule a meeting to prepare a living Trust & Will
2. Pay for someones food behind me and look for ways to pay it forward
3. Purchase new gratitude journals

Day 3 Tasks - Today I will complete these three task by 9:00pm

1. Wash my car
2. Pick up my dry cleaning
3. Work on Business logos

Day 4 Tasks - Today I will complete these task by 9:00pm

1. Get pampered - Hair & Nails & Spa
2. Attend a Womans Network happy hour - grow Networth
3. Find one new Distributor

Day 5 Tasks - Today I will complete these three task by 9:00pm

1. Drop dog off at day spa
2. Pay bills
3. Explore investment with boxable

Day 6 Tasks - Today I will complete these three task by 9:00pm

1. Go to pool
2. Mail out Tea orders
3. Walk the dog

Day 7 Tasks - Today I will complete these three task by 9:00pm

1. Praise the Lord with Gratitude We Worship Him
2. Family bbq
3. Work in yard

This is just an example of a weekly task list. It does not need to be difficult to name three things you will accomplish. I always start my day with prayer and get in the habit of making my bed everyday because its the first tasks that was on my list when I started working on my dream declare deliver tasks. It was the easiest thing to get done first. Then I started looking at tasks that align with my goals. I started to challenge myself more.

Its also important to meet with your accountabili-tea' partner or Tea'm at 9:00pm to clear your tasks and declarations.

Are you completing all three tasks or just one or two?

How are your showing up 100%?

Remember Your vibe attracts your tribe.

Integri-Tea' & Hones-Tea' (Dream Declare Deliver)

This is an Intregri-tea' test with yourself. Are you keeping your word?

Take Accountabili-Tea & Responsibil-Tea for keeping your word, actions and choices.

If you find that you are only completing 1 or 2 tasks you are not showing up one hundred percent.

What is causing the gap? Focus, Clear Intension, Not keeping your word.

After focus, add set clear intentions. Remember Hones-Tea is the best Policy in keeping you word with yourself.

Where else is this showing up in your life?

Do it for YOU!!!

From Scarci-Tea' to Financial Responsibili-Tea's

When we live from a place of scarici-tea we will always hold on to a limited belief that we will never have enough.

Move from a scarity mindset to an abundant mindset.

Invest wisely and often

Look at long term and short term investments

Title ten percent (Give our first fruits to the Church) God loves a cheerful giver.

Save ten percent (for Emergencies)

Money is not just about numbers its mindset, how you think, act and decide to invest and protect what matters most.

Have a living Will & Trust to protect your assets

Protect your family with a Life Insurance policy

My belief is we all have a responsibility to manage our finances and give our first fruits to the Lord (He wants us to be rich, he just wants 10%)

Generosi-Tea:

Genorosity from the Lord looks like blessings, favor, and contentment reguardless of the circumstances.

Become a Genorosi-Tea Rock star and give to local churches and Chari-tea's.

Give secretly...The givers sleep better than the takers.

If God gave you the gift of Generosi-Tea' take that opportunity to make a positive impact and be in service. God loves a cheerful giver, therefore, Be in Gratitude when in service. and invest in Gods Kingdom daily.

God loves a cheerful giver be in gratitude when in service.

Invest in Gods kingdom.

Scarci-Tea:

Do not live with a scarcity mindset. Reprogram your MINDSET!

If you think you'll never have enough , you're right!

God tells us to be anxious for nothing.

Grow out of the social pressures and personal set backs that caused trauma around money

Don't worry about anything, instead pray about everything.

Prosperi-Tea':

Invest wisely until you bank account looks like a phone number.

Look at what you have in life that money cant buy... Love , Peace, Joy, etc.

Look at your heart for that's where you true treasure lives.

Its nice to have money in your pockets, but having the lord in your heart is a Million time better.

Transformation Happens Within

15 years ago I went through an emotional intelligence transformational leadership course that changed my life. I learned that my limited beliefs around money and food in a word was Scarcity. I guess I had programmed my mind to believe I would never have enough. The problem is that when you set your mind to a limited belief, it will indeed become limited. When you live from a place of scarcity, you often cannot move forward until you break down that barrier. However, when you come from a place of gratitude and abundance you often gain more of that in your life.

I learned to peel the onion one layer at a time around my limited beliefs and I created goals that would finally allow me to achieve my financial independence, heal my heart from loss and come out with a new transformed mindset.

I had mentors, and leadership coaches. I set small attainable goals on a weekly, monthly and yearly basis. Every day I would Dream, Declare and Deliver as mentioned earlier and would purposely define three tasks each day to get closer to my goals. I was on a 100 day journey to create a habit where I had an accountability Tea'm of six people that would hold me accountable for keeping my word. I would share my three goals by 9:00am every morning. Then I would clear my declarations by 9:00pm every night for one hundred days. It's a test to see if you completed one, two or all three goals on your daily list. It's really an Integri-Tea' issue and test with you keeping your word with yourself. Are you staying true to you? What three things are getting you closer to your big fat juicy goals?

I set out to buy a second home fifteen years ago and I successfully achieved that goal. Saved money for the down payment, found a home that was double the size and double the payment. Fourteen years later I sold that home, and I thanked God for allowing me to have made a wise investment by doubling my investment. My goal is to be debt-free in all areas of life. The Lord truly knows the desire of my heart, because He has put me in a life situation that I have desired for so many years. To truly be debt free, living on a beach and living my best life is truly a dream come true. My lease begins in September 2025' and all I can think of are the many sunrises I get to witness. All while the good Lord watches over me and directs my steps. After all, He was the one to reset my course in life with this blessing. He has blessed me to be a Genorosi-Tea' Rockstar!!!! And live my very best life.

My prayer for you comes with a million Amen's, and a trillion Hallelujah's, for a billion-answered prayer's.

May God walk through your house and take away all your financial woes, pains, worries, illnesses, struggles and sadness. May He move you from poverty to prosperity. May He watch over your family, finances, and loved ones, and heal all who are sick. May He bring peace and possibili-tea', where there is chaos, longivity and strength where there is weakness, a hope and a future where there is despair, light where there is darkness, and above all, may He put love in your heart and blessings in your pocket. Delight yourselves in the Lord, because He will give you the Abili-Tea' to produce wealth that surpasses all understanding. Amen and Amen!! Thank you Jesus!!

When everyone else counted me out, God called me in. He calls me "chosen." He has anointed my head with oil. He provided everything I need and I am forever grateful to Him.

Always remember, Philippians 4:19 says, "My God shall supply all your needs according to His riches in glory."

Luke 6:38 says, "Give and it will be given to you. A good measure and portion, pressed down, shaken, together, and running over." May your Tea cups runneth over.

Erica Elliott

WarriorHeart Healing Hearts
Brain Code Strategist, Counselor, Author & Speaker

https://www.linkedin.com/in/erica-elliott-ms-lpc-b90911150
https://www.facebook.com/warriorheartxo
https://www.instagram.com/warriorheartxo
https://linktr.ee/WarriorHeartxo
https://msha.ke/warriorheartxo

Erica Elliott is a passionate Brain Code Strategist and founder of WarriorHeart Healing Hearts, with over 30 years of experience as a Licensed Counselor and Certified in many different areas. Holding a Master's Degree in Counseling Psychology, she skillfully integrates evidence-based neuropsychological tools, including Neurobiology, NLP, Somatic, EMDR, CTT, CTFT, hypnotherapy, theology and more to help individuals unlock their true potential and reveal their MASTERPIECE.As an acclaimed author and international speaker, Erica captivates audiences by fostering engagement and emotional connection, ensuring participants leave inspired and equipped for personal growth. Through the Masterpiece Project, she is dedicated to transforming lives, empowering individuals to heal, grow, and soar into the extraordinary futures they deserve. Join her on this journey to recode your life for greatness!

Prosper God's Way: A Journey to Freedom, Clarity, and Abundance

By Erica Elliott

It didn't start with a grand idea or a bold move—it started with desperation. I was sick, depleted, and barely making it through the day. COVID had stolen so much—my energy, clarity, and sense of self. Every step felt like walking through mud. My brain was fogged, my body fatigued, and my spirit... well, my spirit was barely hanging on.

Strength had always been my companion. As a counselor for over three decades and a brain health coach, I was no stranger to resilience. My faith had guided me through countless trials. However, nothing could prepare me for the moment when my own body became my adversary. The teachings I had shared with others transformed into the very medicine I now desperately needed. I found myself grappling to establish a new normal, but it felt like an insurmountable challenge.

One fateful day, overwhelmed by exhaustion, I cried out to God—not with eloquent phrases or polished prayers, but with a heartfelt honesty that echoed from the depths of my soul: "God, I can't do this anymore." In that vulnerable moment, I sensed His reply, reminding me of the strength I had offered my daughter during her own battles with illness. Memories flooded my mind—eight years prior, when she nearly succumbed to multi-drug-resistant bacteria. I wanted to argue that my situation was different, yet the truth was stark: This battle was now mine to fight.

I recalled the countless hours I had spent praying over my daughter, declaring healing through God's Word, creating recordings filled with affirmations and meditations for her recovery. I had witnessed her transformation from a state of debilitating illness to a little-by-little healing, to finally, after a few years and battles, being almost free from limitations. The pain she endured, the struggles to walk or engage in normal activities, the difficult decision to homeschool her because of her sickness—it all came rushing back. I remembered the doctor's grim words, stating there was no cure, and the CDC experts who echoed his sentiments, sharing disheartening statistics that loomed over us.

That day is forever imprinted on my heart; I collapsed to my knees, begging God to spare my daughter and take my life instead. Isn't that the instinct of a mother when her love for her child knows no bounds? But God had a different path in store for us. Rather than succumbing to despair, I chose to anchor myself in faith, holding fast to the belief that healing was attainable. I sought His guidance, and in His grace, after hours of diligent research, I discovered that certain tinctures had successfully battled the bacteria at the University of California. The doctor agreed to pursue this promising avenue, and we embarked on a new chapter in our fight.

The journey was long and arduous, but today, my daughter thrives. Aside from a few significant food allergies, she has become a mother herself, with a beautiful child and another on the way. As I reflected on that tumultuous time, I whispered to God, "If this is to be my thorn in the flesh, as Paul experienced, then teach me how to live with it." I hold on to the hope that complete healing is within reach, but even if it is not, I will continue to serve Him faithfully.

And in that surrender, something shifted.

God didn't respond with lightning bolts or sudden healing. No, His answer came in two unfolding journeys—one with my daughter, the other with my husband. One birthed a thriving business. The other birthed a new way of living. Both breathed life back into me.

The first journey began with a phone call to my daughter. She was seven months pregnant, and her husband was deployed overseas. From my own teachings with clients, I knew how difficult being behind four walls can be for your psyche. I said, "What if we go out once a week—just a little outing, a mini vacation? Let's get out of the four walls and try new places out." She was a little apprehensive about trying new food places because of some of her food allergies but loved the idea of exploring new places, like going on mini vacations and vlogging about it.

That one simple yes turned into a series of weekly adventures—coffee shops, boutiques, food spots, laughter, healing. Before we knew it, people were watching, asking us to promote their businesses. And suddenly, we had a company—OklahomaHot Spots. A marketing media business born from our mutual burnout. A miracle in motion.

The second journey started when my husband said he was retiring soon, and since I had to retire from my government job because of my health, he wanted me to think about selling everything and buying a yacht to do the Great Loop. First, I didn't even know what the Great Loop was. And sell everything? Like, could we even do that? Leave our families and do something we've never done. That surrender led us to possibilities of dreaming new dreams, to new adventures... to living on a yacht for a year, building our dream home, and walking into financial freedom, debt-free with more than a million in assets and a new purpose. It was never about the stuff. It was about saying yes to the call of God when everything familiar felt like too much.

These journeys didn't come from hustle. They came from surrender. And through them, God began showing me that prosperity isn't something you chase—it's something you align with. Prosperity God's way flows from the inside out. It's a healing of the heart, a renewing of the mind, and a rewiring of the brain. Romans 12:2 (NIV) reminds us: "Do not conform to the pattern of this world, but be transformed by the renewing of your mind."

What follows are the seven steps God walked me through—biblical, neurological, and personal practices that created freedom and clarity from the inside out. These aren't theories. They are lived truths. They're the process of becoming who God designed you to be.

Step 1: Pause and Breathe

In the early stages of my post-COVID healing, there were days when the only thing I could manage was to breathe. And honestly, even that felt like a battle. I would place my hand over my heart, close my eyes, and whisper, "God, please help me inhale peace and healing and exhale this fear." I had been trained to be strong, to "suck it up and drive on," as we say in the military. But what I had to learn in this season was that strength sometimes looks like softness—like surrendering to the present moment and breathing it in.

Genesis 2:7 says, "Then the Lord God formed a man from the dust of the ground and breathed into his nostrils the breath of life, and the man became a living being." That breath—God's breath—was our origin. And when we pause to breathe with intention, we are reconnecting to the very life force of heaven. It is a moment of realignment, a sacred pause.

From a brain science perspective, breath is powerful. When you breathe deeply and rhythmically, you activate the parasympathetic nervous system—your body's natural rest-and-digest mechanism. It counteracts the fight-or-flight mode that's triggered by stress and trauma. Deep breathing also helps quiet the amygdala, the part of the brain responsible for fear and emotional reactivity, and strengthens activity in the prefrontal cortex, the center for logic, reasoning, and executive decision-making.

Breathing isn't just relaxation—it's neurological reprogramming. When we breathe slowly and intentionally, we send a message to the brain that we are safe. And when the brain feels safe, it opens up to healing.

Breathing isn't a small thing. It's the foundation. It's the way we pause the chaos and invite heaven in. And sometimes, when that's all you can do—it's more than enough to begin your journey to freedom.

Step 2: Notice the Program

It's hard to heal what you don't even know is there. I remember one day, after weeks of feeling like I was making no progress, I found myself crying on the couch again. I had been doing "all the right things," but still felt stuck and so angry at my body for failing me. That's when God dropped a gentle truth into my spirit: "You're still running old programs." That phrase hit me like a wave.

So much of what we do, think, feel, and believe is not conscious. It's patterned. It's programmed. It's rehearsed behavior and belief that was wired into us in childhood, trauma, culture, or experience. And until we notice the program, we'll keep repeating it.

Proverbs 23:7 says, "As a man thinks in his heart, so is he." It doesn't say "as a man thinks in his mind." It says heart—because it's not just about surface thoughts. It's about deep belief systems embedded in your emotional and spiritual core.

From a neuroscience perspective, our brains love patterns. The basal ganglia are the area responsible for habits—whether they're healthy or harmful. If your brain is wired for scarcity, survival, fear, or shame, it will keep repeating those thought loops unless they're interrupted.

The reticular activating system (RAS) also plays a role. It filters the information we notice based on what we believe. If you believe you're not enough, your brain will constantly "prove" that to you by filtering out anything that says otherwise.

You don't have to be controlled by old programming. But you do have to see it first. Awareness is the first miracle.

Step 3: Speak What You Seek

I'll never forget the day I heard myself say, "I'm so tired of being stuck." And instantly, I felt the Holy Spirit say back, "Then stop reinforcing that narrative with your words." Whoa. That one moment shifted everything.

Our words are not just sounds. They're seeds. They plant into our subconscious and into the spiritual realm. They give our minds—and our miracles—directions to follow.

Mark 11:24 says, "Whatever you ask for in prayer, believe that you have received it, and it will be yours." Belief and declaration go hand in hand. You speak, you believe, and you align your life with that truth.

Neurologically, speaking with intention activates the reticular activating system to start filtering your life through the lens of what you declare. It also begins to change your inner self-perception, which creates emotional safety and promotes rewiring of identity over time.

Your voice is a spiritual and neurological weapon. Speak as if it's already done. Because in the Kingdom—it is.

Step 4: Visualize the Victory

Before I ever stood on stage, wrote a book, built a business, or even walked into healing, I saw it in my mind and felt it in my soul. I would close my eyes, not to escape—but to prepare. I imagined myself whole, vibrant, focused, even joyful. I saw myself helping others. I envisioned rooms filled with love, joy, and light. I pictured freedom—and it became a seed of faith inside me. This is actually a tool I learned when I was a young girl. When I was about 12 or 13, after reading the Bible out of desperation, God led me to read the book called *The Power of Positive Thinking* by Norman Vincent Peale. I began using this tool every night with all the things that I wanted to happen in my life. Every one of those things came true except for one, and that one was one of those things that I would say sometimes I thank God for unanswered prayers.

Hebrews 11:1 tells us, "Now faith is the substance of things hoped for, the evidence of things not seen." Visualization is not fantasy. It's the mental rehearsal of God's promises.

God gave Abraham a vision of stars when he had no children. God gave Joseph dreams before any palace. Jesus even endured the cross "for the joy set before Him." Visualization is an act of faith.

From a brain science standpoint, when you visualize vividly, the brain engages the same neural circuits as if it's actually happening. The motor cortex, sensory centers, and emotional processors light up. The body begins to "practice" the experience before it ever arrives. This primes your nervous system and rewires your belief system.

See it until you believe it. Then move like it's already yours.

Step 5: Feel It Fully

A sacred moment happens when you stop running from your emotions and finally sit down with them. For me, it happened late one night, in the quiet, no distractions—just the ache in my chest and the truth I couldn't outrun. I had to feel the grief. The fear. The loss. I had to feel it in order to heal it.

Ecclesiastes 3:4 says there is "a time to weep and a time to laugh, a time to mourn and a time to dance." Most of us want to skip the weeping and get to the dancing. But what you bury alive doesn't die—it grows.

The limbic system, especially the amygdala and hippocampus, stores unprocessed emotional memory. If not released, it keeps the nervous system in a chronic stress loop. But when we feel an emotion fully, name it, breathe into it, and bring it before God, we release it—and make space for joy.

Your emotions are not the enemy. They're invitations to healing.

Step 6: Rewire with Repetition

Rewiring doesn't happen in a weekend. It happens daily. For me, it was declaring Scripture over my life when I didn't feel it. It was praying when I was tired. It was doing breathwork when my anxiety said run. Healing came in layers—through repetition.

Romans 12:2 doesn't just say be transformed. It tells how—"by the renewing of your mind." Renewal is ongoing. Daily. Intentional.

Neuroplasticity is the brain's ability to form new neural pathways. Repetition strengthens those pathways like a trail in the forest. The more you walk it, the clearer it becomes. Eventually, it becomes the default path.

Consistency creates clarity. And clarity rewires destiny.

Step 7: Act in Alignment

Selling everything and starting over wasn't just brave—it was obedience. We didn't have a perfect plan. We had a prompting. And every time we said yes, God met us with provision, guidance, and miracles. Alignment is not just what you believe—it's what you "do" in response to belief.

James 2:17 says, "Faith by itself, if it is not accompanied by action, is dead." Action is the exhale of belief.

When you act in alignment with God's truth, the brain receives feedback that says, "This belief is safe and effective." The prefrontal cortex—your decision-making center—builds stronger executive function and confidence when your actions match your values.

Faith is not passive. It's progressive. And the more you act on truth, the more it becomes your new normal.

If this journey resonated with you, there's so much more waiting.

You can find deeper guidance, more steps to clearing blocks to blessings, and discover the hidden patterns that keep us stuck in various areas of life—mind, body, spirit, relationships, and finances—in my book ***Breath of Heaven – Manifesting God's Way.*** In it, I combine neuroscience, scripture, and healing practices that have helped thousands move from fear to freedom, from stuck to soaring.

I pray this book has blessed you and that you use and share the tools you've learned. I have a book that expands these areas and so much more that will be released in November of 2025 called ***Brain Coding: We Repeat What We Don't Rewire – It's a Program.*** This book will walk you through the deeper science of your thought patterns, habits, emotional coding, and how to build a daily system to live in the fullness of God's design.

If you found this book helpful, may I ask you a favor? Please leave a review on Amazon. Thank you!

As a Brain Code Strategist, I help people rewire with evidence-based tools to rapidly clear the mess and transform your life into the successful Masterpiece you were always created to be! People also love me speaking to their groups and organizations, teaching them tools in a fun, interactive way. Excited to connect and plus find free resources on the link below. I am always adding new tools and links. Be Blessed and Be a Blessing!

With love,
Erica Elliott

Tazz De Souza

Founder of Her ADHD
Creative Business Strategist

https://www.linkedin.com/in/tazz-creative-business-strategist/
https://www.facebook.com/tazzdesouza

I'm Tazz—South African-born, neurospicy to my core, and a mom in a blended family of ten. I've built businesses, burned them down, and rebuilt from the ground up more times than I can count. I know what it's like to push through burnout, to sit on the shower floor wondering how to keep going, and to come out the other side a little messier but a lot more honest. Her ADHD was born out of those moments—the raw, unfiltered ones where I stopped trying to be who the world wanted and started building around who I actually am. These days, I help other neurodivergent women do the same: embrace their quirks, own their chaos, and build lives that make sense for their brains. Because if there's one thing I've learned, it's this: the chaos was never the problem. It was the plan.

Built from Chaos:
My Son, My Spark, and the Unmasked Me

By Tazz De Souza

The Spark (Past)

I didn't come from a straight, polished path—and honestly, I wouldn't want one if I could. I grew up in South Africa, where the rules were rigid, the uniforms were suffocating, and I was always "too much" for every box they tried to stuff me into.

And man, there were so many boxes.

I guess I always struggled a little bit with authority. But it wasn't that I didn't want to listen—I simply didn't believe they had authority over me just because they were older or held a title. I've never been able to stomach people who abuse their power. Back then, I didn't know how to express that—and even if I had, no one wanted to hear it.

So, I got expelled from high school. Not because I was failing (spoiler: I was smart enough to pass even when I didn't show up)—but because I didn't fit their mold. The system didn't know what to do with me, so it pushed me out.

It wasn't the first time, and it wouldn't be the last, that the system decided I was "too much" and found a way to push me out instead of pulling me in.

When you spend your whole life hearing what's "wrong" with you, you learn to adapt. I masked. I shrank myself. And I found other ways to express who I was, even if I didn't understand that's what I was doing.

What I thought then was just my "party persona," I now realize was my escape—a way to exist in a social world without having to truly interact in it. I could disappear into music, into dancing, and for a little while, it quieted my brain. I've loved dance my entire life because it's one of the few places where I've ever felt completely free. Music has a way of soothing me the way nothing else could.

But outside those rare moments of freedom, I learned how to play by rules I didn't believe in, because survival demanded it.

I went to college for tourism, crushed it academically, and for a moment, I started to wonder if maybe it wasn't me who was broken. Maybe it was my environment. Maybe if I just worked hard enough, I could finally outrun the feeling of being "too much" and prove I could be… enough.

But my story was never going to be that simple.

Fathers, Flaws, and Fire

My dad wasn't the kind of father you ran to for comfort. And if you had asked me back then, I would have told you—without hesitation—that he was a narcissist with a drink in his hand. I grew up learning quickly that love came with conditions.

My stepmom once admitted she was jealous of me because my dad loved me—and I was just a kid. What kind of grown woman says that out loud? For years, I found myself competing for his attention without even realizing how deeply wrong that was.

But now, I see it differently. I see a man who was also just a byproduct of his own childhood trauma. A man who didn't know how to love in a way that didn't hurt the people closest to him. And while that doesn't excuse it, it helps me understand it. For a long time, I thought it meant I was unlovable. It bled into every relationship I had, chipped away at my self-worth, and taught me to expect too little from the people I loved.

But life has a way of throwing you unexpected anchors.

My stepdad—my mom's second husband—wasn't perfect, but he was steady. And in a world where "steady" often felt impossible, he was everything. He was a firefighter in South Africa, working 24-hour shifts, grabbing 48 hours off, and then picking up side businesses on top of it. Not just to keep us afloat, but to give us everything we needed and almost everything we wanted.

He didn't talk much about feelings. But he showed up for me. Every single time. And that? That taught me more than words ever could.

My mom has always been a strong woman—fierce, relentless, the kind of woman who can hold a house together with grit and sheer willpower. She was my anchor. But having a steady man in my life, in a world where my dad's chaos made that feel impossible, changed me.

If there's one thing I got from my stepdad, it's this: unshakable work ethic. The kind of drive that makes you push through even when every part of you wants to stop. I didn't know it then, but that work ethic would become one of my greatest weapons later in life.

Immigration and the Fight to Stand

Although there's a lot that happened in between, life didn't really get easier.

I ended up in a very unhealthy, abusive relationship while working in the States. When it finally fell apart, I headed back home to South Africa and found myself a single mom. From day one—even before my son was born—it was just me and him against the world.

He was my spark.

He was everything I didn't even know I was missing. He carried every ounce of the strength, the purpose, and the fire I had buried inside myself, and somehow, just by being there, he lit it up. He was the reason I realized I didn't have the luxury of "someday." I had to figure it out. He was counting on me, and he didn't have anybody else. Sure, I had family—but not as a parent. Not as the person who was supposed to stand in the gap for him.

So, I worked. I built a career in tourism. But no matter how hard I tried, it was never enough. South Africa is a two-income country, and I had one. And one simply wasn't cutting it.

That's when I made the leap.

I sold everything I owned. I left every single person I loved behind. And I packed my life into a suitcase (more like six suitcases, if we're being real). I grabbed my son, and we moved to the United States—naively thinking that a new country would fix everything.

Spoiler alert: It didn't.

Immigration was brutal. My ex-husband—an American citizen—promised to help me with my green card. Then, he backed out. Twice. $30,000 gone. Two years of my life wasted. And still, I wasn't done fighting.

I had no money. No one left to rely on. I had used every resource I possibly had. And still, I couldn't quit.

So, I did what I do best: I figured it out.

I sat down at my dining room table—thirty days straight, drowning in forms, surrounded by piles of paperwork that ate every inch of space—and I did it myself. I'd already spent thousands on lawyers who got me nowhere, but if there's one thing I know how to do, it's find the gaps, nitpick the details, and refuse to stop until it's done.

And I did it. I handled every form, every step, every signature. And I got approved—on my own.

The only reason I don't have my green card today, almost a decade later, is because I refused to compromise my values for a requirement I didn't believe in. And you know what?

I'd do it again.

Because from the very beginning, it wasn't about me—it was about doing what I believed was best for my son.

And that fight—the one I am still living today—taught me something I'll never forget:

I might bend. I might even crack.

But I. DO. NOT. BREAK.

My North Star

Through all of it—the chaos, the exhaustion, the nights I didn't sleep because my brain never shuts off—my son was my constant.

I've failed at plenty of things, but I have never failed at being his mom.

Even when I was working 12–16-hour days, juggling bills, or crying over immigration forms at 3 a.m., he was the reason I got back up the next morning. He was proof that even when the world feels impossible, there's always something worth fighting for.

And if I'm honest, I think he saved me more than I've ever saved him. Because being his mom didn't just give me a reason—it gave me a mirror. It forced me to see myself through his eyes: unstoppable, fierce, and so much more capable than I believed on my worst days.

When I wanted to quit, he was my reminder that quitting wasn't an option. When I felt like I was failing, he reminded me I was still showing up—and that mattered.

Motherhood didn't make me perfect. It didn't make me patient. It didn't suddenly give me some magic ability to hold it all together. What it did was anchor me.

He's the reason I didn't wait for permission.

He's the reason I learned to fight in the dark.

And he's the reason I finally understood this one, undeniable truth:

You don't wait for perfect when little eyes are watching. You figure it out, messy or not.

Because one day, I want him to look back and know—his mom didn't just survive. She built. She bent, she cracked, but she never broke. And because of that, neither will he.

And maybe that's what makes him my true north. Not because he points me in a straight line, but because no matter how chaotic the path, he reminds me which way is home.

The Fire (Present)

I remember the exact moment I hit rock bottom.

It wasn't some glamorous, movie-worthy breakdown—it was me, sitting outside in the dark, perched on the arm of a chair, drinking wine straight from the bottle. My husband came out and found me there, and I told him the words I hadn't even admitted to myself:

"Right now, living feels harder than dying."

That's how deep it went. And the wildest part? No one would have guessed it from the outside. I was still "functioning," still working insane hours, still holding everything together with sheer force of will. But inside? I was gone.

And the truth? I wasn't sleeping. Not "I stayed up late watching Netflix" kind of not sleeping—I mean, my brain never shut off. For years, I thought it was because I was a night owl or because I was hustling harder than everyone else. Now, I know it was ADHD in overdrive, wired to run at full speed until I collapsed.

The Diagnosis That Broke Me—and Freed Me

The ADHD diagnosis came first. And I'll be honest: I didn't know if I wanted to scream or cry. It felt like grief at first. Like I had spent my whole damn life running uphill in a race I didn't even know I was in.

Then came the meds. Adderall.

And if you think the diagnosis was heavy, the judgment was heavier. Suddenly, I had to explain myself to people who didn't even live my life. The stereotypes, the side-eye, the "isn't that just for college kids pulling all-nighters?" crap—it was endless.

At first, though? The meds felt like magic.

I could do everything. I could build, fix, work, and push. But here's the truth no one tells you:

I didn't suddenly have more capacity. I just had a better way of pretending I did.

And that illusion—oh, it's seductive. I bought into it hard. Until the day I didn't.

That was the day I realized I wasn't actually limitless. I was just over-drafting my life—robbing tomorrow's energy to survive today. And eventually? The account ran dry.

Faith, Grace, and the Shift

Somewhere in the middle of the chaos, faith snuck back in. Not the version I grew up with—the polished, rule-following, "wear the right clothes to church" version. No, this was different.

I stopped listening to people and started listening to God. I stopped asking, "Why me?" and started realizing maybe, just maybe, I wasn't broken. Maybe I was built this way on purpose.

And it wasn't neat or pretty. I didn't have a "hallelujah" moment where everything clicked. Some days it was just me, ugly-crying in the shower, begging God to meet me where I was—and He did. Not with lightning bolts or burning bushes, but with quiet reminders that I was still here. That I was built for this.

And once I stopped fighting it, I started noticing grace everywhere—in the way people I loved showed up for me, in the rare quiet moments that reminded me I was still here, and eventually, in how I learned to show it to myself.

Over-Giving, Undercharging, and the Burnout That Followed

Here's what no one tells you about passion: if you're not careful, it'll eat you alive.

I poured everything I had into my business. I supported my clients like they were family. I undercharged, over-delivered, and told myself I was just "serving." But in reality?

I was building everyone else up while quietly tearing myself down. And here's the thing no one talks about: when you tie your worth to how much you can give, you forget you're a person, too. I was giving discounts I couldn't afford, saying yes when I should've said no, and calling it "service." In reality, I was bleeding out in the name of being "enough."

And for a while, I convinced myself that was noble. That it was what good women—good mothers—did. But all it did was hollow me out.

From One Kid to Eight

And then came the shift that broke me wide open: marrying my husband and going from one kid in my house... to eight.

If anyone ever asks me what shocked me most about becoming part of a family of ten, I won't say the noise or the chaos. I won't even say the laundry (although, holy crap, the laundry).

It's the emotional space.

The sheer bandwidth it takes to hold space for eight kids is… enormous. Bigger than any one human, no matter how determined or caffeinated or "driven," can possibly manage.

And two years ago? I would've sworn it was possible.

I would've told you I just needed to try harder, hustle more, stop being "lazy."

Now? I know better.

You can't outwork impossible.

Burning It Down to Build Again

Before the burnout came the hustle.

For years, I ran my own agency. I scaled it from two contractors to a team of twenty. I managed twenty clients at once. I've had months when I made more money than I knew what to do with, and I've had months when I was staring at my bank account wondering how the hell I was going to make it work.

And honestly? I was obsessed. I wore "busy" like a badge of honor. I chased this shiny version of success that looked good on paper but left me hollow inside.

Even as I blended my family—going from one child to a family of ten—I refused to slow down. I told myself I could do it all. Business. Marriage. Motherhood. Emotional space for eight kids. I thought sheer determination could stretch me enough to hold it all.

But it couldn't.

Slowly, I started to feel it. That whisper that maybe I couldn't keep running like this forever. That maybe my family needed me more than my business did. For years, I wrestled with it. Should I close Founding Females Academy? Should I get a job? Should I keep pushing harder?

And then, it happened.

Burnout didn't just knock me down—it burned away every ounce of bullshit I'd been carrying.

I shut down Founding Females Academy. I let go of the version of success I thought I "should" want.

And here's the truth: Her ADHD didn't come from one big, dramatic "aha" moment. It wasn't lightning-bolt inspiration. It was paper cuts. Years of watching women burn themselves out the same way I had. Years of being told I was "too much" while I quietly held everything together for everyone else. Years of carrying the weight of it all until it crushed me.

And then, in the middle of the rubble—sitting on the shower floor with my head in my hands—Her ADHD was born.

Not as a business plan. Not as some shiny "big idea."

It was survival.

It was me deciding that if I was going to keep going, it had to be different this time. I had to stop building my life around the version of me I thought the world wanted and start building around the version of me that actually existed.

And this is what I've learned:

Burnout didn't just almost break me. It built me.

It stripped me down to the raw, unpolished truth and forced me to rebuild—not in spite of my chaos, but because of it.

And for the first time in my life, I'm not ashamed of that. Because maybe the point was never to "fix" myself. Maybe it was to burn down every version of me that was never mine to begin with—and rise from it, unmasked, unpolished, and finally free.

The Unmasked Future (Becoming)

Her ADHD wasn't born in one single, cinematic moment.

It didn't come with fireworks or some "aha" epiphany where everything suddenly made sense.

It came from a thousand small cracks.

Paper cuts that bled into late nights.

Watching women grind themselves to dust while I over-gave, undercharged, and convinced myself that was noble. Holding a business together, holding a household together, holding myself together—until there was nothing left to hold.

And then one day, sitting on the shower floor with my head in my hands, I realized: I wasn't just exhausted.

I was done.

But I didn't quit.

I rebuilt.

Because if I was going to keep going, it couldn't be the same way. It couldn't be about proving myself or hustling for worth I already had. It couldn't be about chasing someone else's version of "success."

For the first time in my life, I built something for me—not for who I thought I should be, not for what the world expected, but for the raw, messy, unmasked version of me.

And that's how Her ADHD was born.

Not as a business plan.

Not as a polished idea.

But as a rebellion.

Redefining Prosperity

For years, I thought prosperity was reserved for women who could do it all—flawlessly. The six-figure launches. The perfect schedules. The homes that looked like they were ripped out of Pinterest.

And I tried to be her. God knows, I tried.

But none of it mattered until I stopped chasing the version of success that wasn't mine.

Now?

Prosperity looks different.

It's not about endless growth—it's about sustainable growth.

It's paying myself first without guilt.

It's running my business in a way that doesn't cost me my sanity or my family.

It's having enough margin in my life to breathe, to think, to live.

That's the thing nobody tells you: You don't have to burn yourself out to build a life that works. You don't need to hustle harder—you need to stop apologizing for building it differently.

Faith in Every Step

If you're waiting for me to tell you there was one single moment where God flipped the switch and everything made sense—there wasn't.

It wasn't one moment.

It was every moment.

It was the quiet reminder that I'd made it this far through storms that should've swallowed me whole. It was the realization that there was no logical explanation for my survival except for Him.

Faith, for me, isn't neat or polished.

It's messy.

It's loud.

It's crying in the shower and still believing.

And sometimes, it's choosing to trust Him even when I don't get the answers I want.

That's what rebuilt me—not just as a business owner, but as a person.

Redefining What Success Looks Like

For the longest time, I held on so tightly to being a business owner because it felt like my proof.

Proof that I was strong.

Proof that I was capable.

Proof that I was worthy.

But the truth? That grip almost killed the very thing I loved about it.

This year, I finally gave myself permission to loosen that grip. I picked up a role with a company whose mission I believe in—work that doesn't just pay the bills but actually lights me up. And for the first time in years, I could breathe.

Because here's what I've learned: You don't have to white-knuckle your way through entrepreneurship to "make it." Sometimes, prosperity looks like taking the pressure off. Sometimes, it looks like creating stability in one area so you can rebuild in another.

And none of that means you've failed. It means you've evolved.

When I stopped equating my worth with whether or not I could carry it all alone, I realized something even bigger: I don't have to prove I can do it all to deserve what I've built.

Getting my autism diagnosis didn't break me either. It grounded me. It explained why I experience the world the way I do—and it gave me permission to stop fighting my wiring and start building a life that actually works with it.

And if that makes me "too much" for anyone?

Good.

Tell them to put on a damn pair of shades—because I'm done dimming my light just to make other people comfortable.

The Environment Shift

Here's the truth most people won't say out loud: Sometimes, it's not you.

Sometimes, it's your environment.

I spent so many years convinced I was the problem—too much, too scattered, too intense—until I realized I was just trying to bloom in toxic soil.

When I changed my environment—physically, emotionally, spiritually—I didn't magically "fix" myself. I didn't need fixing. What I found was space. Space to see that I was never broken in the first place.

Now? I build my own damn container.

One that fits me—and every other woman who's tired of shrinking to fit into a box she was never made for.

The Next Step (And the One After That)

If there's one thing I've learned, it's this:

It's not about the first step.

It's about the second.

And the third.

And the seventeenth.

And the one you take after you've collapsed on the floor and sworn you're done.

Life isn't one giant leap—it's a series of messy, imperfect, defiant steps forward.

And every single one of mine—from South Africa to single motherhood, to running my agency, to burning it all down and building Her ADHD—has led me here.

No, it's not neat. No, it's not perfect. But it's mine.

And if there's one thing I want you to hear, it's this:

You are allowed to rebuild as many times as it takes.

You are allowed to stop fighting your brain and start building with it.

You are allowed to succeed in a way that actually feels like living.

The chaos was never the problem.

It was the plan.

And now?

I wouldn't trade it for anything.

Elizabeth Meigs

Elizabeth Inspires

https://www.linkedin.com/in/elizabethinspires
https://www.facebook.com/ElizabethMeigsInspires
https://www.instagram.com/elizabethmeigsinspires
https://elizabethinspires.com/
https://blog.elizabethinspires.com/

Elizabeth Meigs, known as the Miracle Power™ Empowerment Coach, Best-Selling Author, and Founder of Elizabeth Inspires. She empowers high-achieving women struggling with burnout, emotional exhaustion, stress, and overwhelm to gain the confidence, clarity, and courage to reclaim their power and pursue their purpose. As the creator of the Pathway to P.E.A.C.E. Method™ and the 8-Week Pathway to PEACE™ Group Coaching Program, Elizabeth combines faith and practical strategies to help women break free from cycles of confusion and emotional chaos. Rooted in her personal journey—overcoming a traumatic brain injury, workplace toxicity, and a toxic marriage—Elizabeth equips others with tools to protect their peace, rise above adversity, and live aligned with their God-given calling. Her mission is anchored in H.O.P.E.—Healing that Opens Pathways to Empowerment. Ready to double your peace and joy? Book your free 30-minute Double Your PEACE & Joy Discovery Call today!

Walking by Faith, Living in Fullness

By Elizabeth Meigs

Have you ever felt like you were holding the pieces of your life together with nothing but your bare hands and a whisper of hope? Like you're showing up for the world—but at times, you're unraveling on the inside?

What about the dreams on your heart? Ever wondered if the dreams on your heart are even possible?
Maybe you've felt invisible. Maybe you've poured everything into others while silently falling apart. Maybe you've looked at your life and thought, *This isn't how it was supposed to go.*

If that's you—I want you to know something:
You are not alone.
I've been there.

At 14, I went from being a small-town dreamer chasing a music career, with my voice as my identity, to fighting for my life in a hospital bed. A traumatic brain injury left me voiceless, broken, and barely alive. The doctors gave me less than a 25% chance of survival. And even when I survived, I didn't feel like I had. I watched life move on without me—while I felt stuck, unseen, and unsure of who I was anymore.

But somewhere in that silence, God whispered:
"I have a plan for you. You can't stop. You have to keep going."

That was the beginning of everything.
Because in that moment, I realized something that would change the entire trajectory of my life:

Prosperity isn't the absence of pain—it's what happens when you say yes to God, even in the midst of it.

I've learned to stop waiting for life to look "possible" before I move.
Because walking by sight will always keep you stuck.
But walking by faith? That's where the miracles live.

I didn't always know where I was going. I just knew I couldn't quit.
And every time I trusted that still, small voice... doors opened.
Healing came. Strength returned.
Prosperity didn't begin in my bank account.
It began in my soul.

So, before we go any further, I want to ask you again:
Where in your life have you felt like giving up?
Where are you still waiting for permission to rise?

Because this chapter isn't just my story—it's yours, too.
It's about learning to walk by faith when nothing makes sense.
It's about embracing the mystery in the journey of life—because that's where the beauty is.

What I'm about to share with you is more than a testimony. It's a divine shortcut. These are the exact tools God gave me to turn breakdowns into breakthroughs—and today, He's calling me to give them to you.

Through God's grace, I created the **Roadmap to Resilience™** and the **Pathway to PEACE™ Method**—tools that took me from surviving to thriving, from stuck to soaring, and from invisible... to influential.

And here's what I've realized: I wasn't just providing hope to others over the past 13 years—I've been *delivering healing*, heart, mind, and soul. And now, I walk boldly in that purpose. Not because of who I am, but because of *who He is in me*.

You're not reading this by accident.
God is reaching out His hand, calling you to rise—just as He did for me.

Let's begin this journey together—**from Possibility... to Prosperity.**

But first, I have to take you to the moment where it all could've ended.

I was down on my knees, begging God to take me. Not out of rebellion—but because I truly believed everything would be easier if I were no longer here. I couldn't see a way out. I felt like an ugly monster, unlovable and forgotten. I was drowning in isolation and silently unraveling in a world that had moved on without me.

Have you ever felt that kind of invisible pain? The kind that makes you question your worth... your purpose... your existence?

If so, I want you to hear me clearly:
You can't stop. You have to keep going.
Because there is a *much greater plan* for your life—just like there was for mine.

In that darkest hour, when I had nothing left, God reached out with His voice of Hope:
"I have a plan for you. You can't stop. You have to keep going."

It completely overwhelmed my heart and soul; I felt His love surrounding me.

That moment didn't erase the pain.
But it planted a seed.
A seed of *perspective.*
A seed of *purpose.*

Suddenly, it wasn't just about my pain anymore. It was about the people He was calling me to help. The thought of someone else hurting—even half as much as I was—broke me even deeper. But it also gave me fuel. I became determined to be for someone else what I so desperately needed in that moment:
A voice of light in the darkness.

It was in that weakness that I first felt true strength.
Not mine—**His**.

"But he said to me, 'My grace is sufficient for you, for my power is made perfect in weakness.' Therefore I will boast all the more gladly about my weaknesses, so that Christ's power may rest on me. (...) *For when I am weak, then I am strong."*
— 2 Corinthians 12:9-10 (NIV)

I didn't have a plan. I didn't have clarity.
But I had a promise.
So, I began doing the only thing I could—**praising through the pain**.

Every night, I thanked God.
Not for the trauma—but for being *with me* in it.
I thanked Him for the seed of purpose He had planted in my soul. For reminding me that if I still had breath, I still had a reason. That simple act of gratitude became my reset. It rewired my mind long before I understood the science behind it. And it gave me strength to rise.

Here's what I want you to know:

Perspective gives you power.

But when you're buried under chaos and confusion, it's hard to see the bigger picture. That's why we need support. That's why we need tools to help us reframe our pain. Because what you focus on grows; we must learn to shift those negatives into positives, and that was exactly what I was doing through His grace and mercy.

What I learned was this:

You can't wait to feel strong to move.

You move—and that's when strength shows up.

It's not found in the waiting.

It's found in the walking.

Breakthrough doesn't come when you feel ready.

It comes when you *refuse to stay stuck.*

Momentum doesn't follow comfort.

It follows commitment.

And every step you take in faith—no matter how shaky—builds the strength you thought you didn't have.

If you want to see the impossible become possible, you have to stop waiting for perfect conditions—and start trusting the One who makes a way through them.

Through God's grace and mercy, I began developing tools and strategies to move from surviving to thriving. What I didn't realize at the time is that I was already walking in the early steps of what would become my **Roadmap to Resilience™**—a Spirit-led framework that has helped me, and now many others, shift from despair to destiny.

And you? You're not reading this by accident.

If life feels like chaos, if you've been stuck in survival mode—mentally, emotionally, or spiritually—**you're not broken. You're under construction.**

You don't fight this hard for nothing.
You feel resistance because there is *great value* in you.
I want to let you in on a little secret:

Thieves don't break into empty houses.

The enemy only attacks what is full of purpose.

So yes, it's going to take work. It will take surrender.
But **a heart transformation** is how you move from pain to purpose, from broken to rebuilt, from stuck to prosperous.

You were meant for greatness.
But you must be willing to heal from the inside out—**to be rebuilt, renewed, and restored** into who God created you to be.

I know it's not easy.
But nothing worth doing in life ever is.

And I'm standing here to tell you: **You've got this. I believe in you.** Belief and faith are the catalysts to all great things in life. You can't let this world take that away from you, and today you are receiving the very tools to reclaim your power to pursue your purpose.
He is calling you to rise.

I made it through high school by God's grace and mercy.
College, though? That was no cake walk.

I still faced judgment and rejection—but something had changed.

This time, it didn't break me.
By then, my confidence had grown.
So had my courage.

And even on the days I didn't feel like moving forward, I kept showing up. One foot in front of the other. No spotlight. No clarity. Just quiet, obedient movement.

And something powerful began to happen in that process:
I was gaining vision.

It was through *reflection* that I began to see that maybe—just maybe—everything I had walked through was working together for good.

The missteps.
The detours.
The closed doors.
The hard lessons.
All of it.

Even when I didn't fully understand my purpose, I could sense it was being formed inside of me. I was starting to trust the process—not just believe in it.

Yes, I made wrong turns.
Yes, I took some paths I wish I hadn't.
But each one was building something in me: resilience, wisdom, and a deeper understanding of who I was becoming.

Twelve years after the night my world was ripped apart, I graduated with an associate's degree in Occupational Therapy.

That moment?
That was when everything clicked.

Because when I walked into my very first patient's room—a stroke survivor who had lost all hope—I knew why I had to go through what I did.

As I sat across from them, I shared my story.
And I watched something shift in their eyes.
Hope.

That's when I knew:
God wasn't just healing me—He was answering a prayer I had whispered for over a decade.

I used to beg God, *"Please be the same voice of Hope on others' hearts who feel defeated and overwhelmed, wanting to give up… the way You were on mine."*

And now—He was; I had become His messenger.

Reflection reveals what you can't see in the middle of the storm.

I didn't know it then, but every delay had a purpose.
Every unanswered question was preparing me for a greater calling.
Every no was making space for a divine yes.

And you, too, are being prepared—even when it feels like nothing is happening.

God is always listening.
He hasn't forgotten you.
He's shaping you in the silence.

In His perfect timing, God will align every step, every lesson, every delay—to elevate you into the next phase of your destiny

So, don't despise the waiting.
Honor it.

Because reflection doesn't just bring healing.
It brings strategy.
And strategy brings clarity.

You are not behind.
You are right on time for what God is building in you.

I've learned something powerful through the rediscovery phases of my life:
When things begin to feel chaotic again...
When confusion clouds my clarity...
That's not a sign to shut down.
It's a divine signal to **move.**

Because often, **confusion is the cue that growth is calling.**
It's another invitation to rise.
And rising again takes willingness. It takes courage.
It requires stepping out in faith—even when you don't feel ready.

But here's the truth I need you to hear:
You were created and equipped to do exactly that.

The dreams on your heart?
The vision you carry for your life?
They're not random.
They're not a coincidence.
They are **divine assignments**—strategic whispers from Heaven pointing you toward your purpose.

And today, I want to challenge you to shift:
Start living like those dreams were placed inside you **on purpose**—because they were.

They're not just ideas.
They're the **roadmap to your resilience.**
And they hold the key to a peace this world can't offer.

But here's the part most people miss:
They will feel impossible—**until you surrender them to the Source.**

For me, that's what **prosperity** truly is.
It's not about money, fame, or fortune.
It's about living the life you were *created* for—where you lack for nothing.
Where you're supplied daily with **strength, peace, joy, and fulfillment.**

That kind of prosperity comes from alignment.
From walking hand-in-hand with the One who gave you the vision in the first place.

And the greatest reward?
It's not a platform. It's not applause.
It's being able to help others who are where I once was.
Those who want to believe.
Those who want to heal.
Those who feel the call—but don't know how to answer it.

That's why I do what I do.

But I couldn't step into this without first letting go.

I had to release what was holding me back.
The regrets.
The shame.
The "what ifs."
The need to control how it all unfolded.

Once I did that?
The sky became the limit. My Impossible was becoming I'm Possible!

I share this because the same can be true for you.
Your rediscovery begins when you lay down the lies and pick up the truth of who God says you are.
You're not too far gone.
You're not too late.
You are still becoming.

And every step you take toward healing is a step back into your **true power, purpose, and peace.**

So how do you begin this journey for yourself?
That's where Reconnect comes into play.

Throughout this chapter, I've walked you through how I learned to reconnect with my Source (God), my voice, and the woman He created me to be.
But I would have never arrived here if I hadn't first been willing to **grow** into her.

The truth is, growth requires movement.
It requires letting go of people, patterns, and places that no longer align with God's plan for your life.
And as you grow, some things will fall away—not to harm you, but to make room for the **abundance God is trying to give you**.

In 2017, God began to show me what happens when someone truly sees you.

I met a friend who saw my heart—and believed in me. He saw me through God's eyes. His belief became a mirror that helped reflect my value, before I fully saw it in myself. That moment marked the beginning of my boldness on stage. I began to speak hope into rooms filled with people who felt like I once did—lost, stuck, unseen.

At the time, I didn't understand the "why" behind it all.
But God made it clear: **"I brought you two together to bring you both closer to Me."**

And in my humanity, I laughed.
I thought I was already close to God—I was leading in church, walking in faith, doing all the right things.
But now I see: **God wasn't just calling me closer in action—He was preparing me for a battle I never saw coming.**

Because when I later found myself in a toxic marriage, constantly being told that the dreams on my heart were foolish and they would never come true—I remembered what it felt like to be seen, supported, and celebrated.

That memory, along with God's promise, kept me from believing the lies.
My purpose had already taken root.
I had already begun to flourish.
So, I clung tight to the promise God gave me years earlier.
And He began to surround me—again—with people who lifted me up, affirmed my calling, and reminded me that my voice still mattered.

Then came the divine rescue.

On Easter weekend, 2023—Resurrection Sunday—God made a way of escape.

He spoke clearly: **"If you're going to fulfill My will, you can't stay here."**

So, I moved.
Not because I had it all figured out.
But because I had the faith to *seek* His way forward.

"Ask and it will be given to you; seek and you will find; knock and the door will be opened to you."
— Matthew 7:7 (NIV)

And when I sought Him—**He met me**.
When I moved—**He moved greater**.
When I stepped into uncertainty—**He flooded me with peace.**

That peace came rushing back the moment I left the chaos.
It was like a breath I didn't know I had been holding.

In the weeks that followed, God brought something full circle.

He brought clarity to me about the exact strategies I had developed during my brain injury recovery. He whispered, **"Had you not developed these strategies, you would not have survived your marriage."**

That's when it clicked:
These same strategies had helped me overcome trauma, burnout, toxic workplaces, and emotional exhaustion.
And now, He was calling me to teach them.

So, I created the **Pathway to PEACE™ Method**—a biblical, practical, Spirit-led foundation for emotional and spiritual alignment.

And then He gave me language for the journey I had lived:
The **Roadmap to Resilience™**.

But as I walked it out... I realized it was more than resilience.
It was righteousness.
It was alignment with God's will, ways, and Word.
It was the exact path Jesus walked—death to resurrection, pain to purpose.

He rescued me on *Resurrection Sunday* to make that truth known:
What was meant to bury you is what God will use to raise you.

So whatever challenge you're facing today—
Whatever chaos, heartbreak, or hopelessness you're holding onto—
I want you to know:

You don't have to wait 25 years like I did.

I've given you the shortcut.
The map.
The miracle.

You have the tools now:
Rise. Reframe. Reflect. Rediscover. Reconnect.

This is how you move from stuck... to soaring.
From striving... to surrender.
From survival... to **supernatural strength, or Miracle Power™ as God informed me I had stepped fully into in October of 2024.**

This is how you move from **Possibility... to Prosperity.**

And prosperity?

It's not just provision.

It's **peace**.

It's **purpose**.

It's walking in **divine alignment** where your needs are supplied and your soul is fulfilled.

Friend, this is your invitation.

Don't just survive.

Rise. Reconnect. Rebuild.

You were never meant to stay stuck.

You were created to **prosper**.

And when you stop trying to control the outcome—and start trusting the One who already sees the full picture—**you'll discover a life more beautiful than anything you could imagine.**

Let this be the day you say yes.

Let this be the day you rise.

Latraila Tolbert

Essential HER Solutions
Strategic Revenue Consultant

https://www.linkedin.com/in/latraila-tolbert/
https://www.instagram.com/essentialhersolutions/
https://essentialhersolutions.com/
https://milliondollarstrategy.co/

Latraila Tolbert is a strategic business architect for powerhouse women entrepreneurs ready to scale beyond six figures without adding more to their calendar. With 20 years of operational leadership and 7 years in the online space, she helps high-performing founders optimize what they've already built and accelerate sustainable, intelligent growth. After launching Essential HER Solutions in 2017, her business took on new meaning when her youngest son was diagnosed with leukemia. From hospital rooms, she designed the frameworks that allowed her to sustain five-figure months while staying present for her family, proving that strategy can create freedom, not just revenue. Through her Revenue Psychology Framework™ and strategic evolution methodology, she's helped clients restructure for scale, like guiding a $40K/month attorney to $85K, and helping a six-figure consultant cross the million-dollar mark by restructuring instead of starting over. Tea-drinking strategist. Mom of three. Quiet force behind your next level.

The Aligned Path: Turning What You Love into Lasting Profit

By Latraila Tolbert

When the Quiet Got Loud

It was a Tuesday night in early September 2017.

The kind of night when all you want is silence.

The boys had finally finished up their homework and went off to bed. My husband had called it an early night. And for the first time since I got home from work, the house was quiet.

I sat at our dining table, a hot mug of spiced apple tea beside my laptop. The crisp scent of apple and cinnamon reminds me that fall is near, grounding me as I stare next to my laptop, staring at a blank Google document titled *My Business Plan*.

For months, I'd been having this idea that wouldn't let me go. It was there when I cooked dinner. It followed me to work. It called to me while I was cleaning the house.

I wanted to help women like me, women with skills, experience, and ambition, who were constantly told "no" but had no clear path to turn what they knew into income they could count on.

But instead of writing out my plan, I was doing what I'd been doing for months: stalling.

Reading through yet another "How to Start Your Business" article. Making a fresh list of all the things I told myself I needed before I could *really* start a polished logo, a perfect website, professional photos, and a full content plan.

The truth? I wasn't preparing. I was hiding.

Because as long as I stayed in the planning phase, I couldn't fail. But I also couldn't move forward.

That night, something shifted. I couldn't tell you if it was frustration, exhaustion, or the quiet finally giving me the space to hear myself clearly. But my fingers started moving.

I typed one sentence:

"I help women turn their knowledge into income."

That was it. No perfect elevator pitch. No color-coded business model. Just one line that felt *true*.

That messy little sentence became the seed for Essential HER, the business that has since guided over 300 women, from attorneys and bookkeepers to coaches and creatives, to design scalable revenue streams and step into their authority as entrepreneurs.

It also gave me the lesson I've built my business and my life on:

Action beats perfection. Every single time.

The Clarity to Cash Framework

Before we go further, I want to give you the roadmap I wish I'd had back at that dining room table. Because clarity without action is paralyzing, and action without clarity is chaos.

Through working with over 300 women business owners, I discovered a pattern: The ones who grew quickly and sustainably moved through five key stages I call the **Clarity to Cash Framework:**

1. **Get Clear on Your Zone of Genius**
    Your mix of skills, experiences, and perspectives is your unfair advantage. Write it down. Own it.

    Action Step: Write one sentence about what comes easiest to you that others constantly ask you for.

2. **Identify Your Ideal Impact**
   Define the transformation you create and who you most want to serve.

   Action Step: Write a "before and after" for your dream client, what changes for them because of you?

3. **Start Before You're Ready**
   Launch a simple offer, what I call a *minimum viable offer,* and let the market teach you.

   Action Step: Identify one problem you can solve in under 90 minutes and offer it to five people this month.

4. **Listen and Iterate**
   Use every client interaction as data to refine your process.

   Action Step: After each client session, jot down what worked, what confused them, and what lit them up.

5. **Build Your Scalable Foundation**
   Document what works. Turn it into repeatable systems and scalable offers.

   Action Step: Pick one thing you do repeatedly and write down the exact steps. That's the start of your first scalable asset.

This framework is the tried and true path of my journey, and the journey of every client I've walked with since. Keep it in your back pocket as we go.

The Decision to Stop Asking for Permission

There comes a moment when you realize the recognition you've been waiting for isn't coming and that continuing to play small only delays your own future. For me, that moment became the line in the sand: stop asking for permission, and start leading on my own terms.

Before I became an entrepreneur, I spent over 20 years in operations and project management. I was the one people called when things needed to run smoothly. I lead teams, managed complex launches, and kept departments from crumpling.

Seven of those years were in the online business world, where leaders had big visions but needed someone like me to keep projects from falling apart.

And yet... every time I applied for a leadership role, I got the same answers:

> "You don't have enough experience."
> "It's not your time yet."
> "You need certifications to do the work you're already doing."

I remember one moment vividly. I was in a conference room, presenting a project I was brought on at the last minute. The room was full of men in suits. They nodded at my results, complimented my work, and then announced that someone else would be promoted into the role I had essentially been performing for months.

I sat there with a polite smile, but inside I felt the air leave my chest.

I was tired of proving myself in rooms where my value was obvious. Tired of being passed over while my work spoke for itself. Tired of asking for opportunities instead of creating them. I was done asking for permission to lead.

When my position was relocated to North Carolina, I finally admitted that something was clear to me: I wasn't going with them.

Walking away wasn't just a career move. It was a declaration. It was my chance to go all in.

But I had one non-negotiable: I would build something that no one could take away from me.

The Truth About Turning Passion Into Profit

So many women think profit requires a brand-new idea or a moment of genius. The truth is simpler: your profit often lies in what's already in your hands, the skills and experiences you've been overlooking.

Entrepreneurship loves to romanticize the "aha moment." That lightning bolt idea that changes everything overnight.

That's not reality..

Turning your passion into profit isn't about inventing something new. It's about recognizing the value of what's already in your hands.

That "thing" you do so naturally, you almost overlook it? That's your advantage.

For me, it wasn't just a "business strategy." It was my ability to take a scattered vision, a messy list a mile long, and turn it into a streamlined, step-by-step plan that actually got results.

The question that unlocked everything for me was:

What do people already come to me for?

When I answered honestly, strategy, systems, and scaling, I stopped chasing shiny ideas and built on my strengths.

Your passion lives where three things meet:

1. What you love
2. What you're naturally good at
3. What people are willing to pay for

And here's the good news: You don't need to have all three perfectly defined before you start. Begin with one or two. Let the rest reveal itself as you take action.

Up to that point, I had been building my business on what would later become my Clarity to Cash Framework. Getting clear on my strengths, defining the impact I wanted to make, and testing simple offers in real time. But nothing tests your systems and your resolve like life itself. When everything shifted with my son's diagnosis, that framework stopped being just strategy; it became my lifeline.

When Life Forces a Pivot: The Messy Middle

Every business journey has a season where nothing goes as planned. The messy middle isn't the end; it's the place where you're reshaped, and where resilience teaches you to build differently.

For me, the messy middle came in 2019, my second year of business. Things were moving forward; I had clients, momentum, and a plan.

And then my youngest son was diagnosed with Leukemia.

Everything stopped.

I can still remember that first night in the hospital. A room full of doctors and nurses surrounded us, explaining what the next 30 days would look like. I watched in shock as the nurse hooked my baby boy up to IVs and drew his blood, the air in the room so cold it felt like it was pressing against my skin. By nightfall, I collapsed onto the thin sofa bed, listening to the constant sound of doors opening and closing up and down the hall, the cries of other children echoing in the background. My husband and I held each other's fear quietly, replaying every moment in our minds, asking if we'd missed any signs and praying, over and over, that our little boy would make it through.

In those days, I couldn't leave the hospital for hours, sometimes days. My husband had less flexibility at work, so I stayed. I even helped our older son with homework over a video call from that uncomfortable, hard sofa bed.

That season of constraint forced me to rebuild my business differently, so I created:

- **Digital Frameworks:** I couldn't be live with clients all the time; there were constant tests, nurses, and staff flowing in and out, so I started creating frameworks my clients could work through on their own.
- **VIP Days**: I couldn't commit to long-term, tight schedules, so I restructured my offers into VIP Days. These focused sessions gave me the flexibility to serve deeply while maintaining financial stability.
- **Automation:** With no team and no capacity to manage endless admin tasks, I automated everything I could so the business could run even when I wasn't available.

What could have ended my business became the reason I built something more sustainable, something that could carry me and my clients through the hardest season of my life.

The Power of Small, Aligned Steps

Big leaps look exciting from the outside, but it's the quiet, consistent steps that create a sustainable business. Every aligned action, even the small ones, compounds into real impact.

Here's what my first year *really* looked like:

Month 1: Wrote my one-sentence offer and told my husband. I posted it on LinkedIn and Facebook. Saying it out loud made it real.

Month 2: Three women reached out. I had no packages, so I offered to work with them for free in exchange for feedback.

Month 3: I noticed I was repeating myself, so I turned my process into a one-page framework. That became my first paid offer.

Months 4–5: Sold my 90-minute session plus framework to my warm network. I focused on conversations, not content calendars.

Month 6: Turned my repeated one-on-one sessions into a group program, five women, one Zoom room, and a four-week curriculum.

Months 7–12: Ran that group program repeatedly, refining it each time until it became my signature framework.

Those steps weren't flashy. But they built trust, results, and confidence - the foundation for everything that came later.

Winning the Inner Game

The strategies matter, but your mindset decides if they'll work. Learning to challenge the voice of doubt and lead with courage is what unlocks the next level of growth.

The biggest challenge isn't strategy. It's the voice in your head whispering:

> *"You're not ready."*
> *"You're not qualified.*
> *"It's been done before."*

I've heard that voice too.

Here's how I flipped the script:

- From "I'm not qualified" to "I'm uniquely qualified."
- From "It's been done before" to "It hasn't been done by me."
- From "I need to know everything" to "I need to know enough."
- From "I can't fail" to "I can't not try."

Confidence doesn't come first. Courage does.

The Ripple Effect of Courage

When you take bold, aligned action, you're not just changing your own life. You give permission for others, clients, peers, and even your family to step into their own power, too.

Take Sarah.

She is a brilliant attorney stuck in a traditional law firm. She loved the work but hated the grind. Long hours, little flexibility, no ownership of her schedule. She feared leaving her "secure" paycheck, and doubted whether clients would come if she struck out on her own.

Together, we built a consulting practice around her expertise: legal strategy for women entrepreneurs. We designed her first offer, mapped her onboarding, and created a referral system.

Her first client came within weeks. Within two years, Sarah was earning more than she ever had at her firm, and doing it on her own terms. More than that, she was helping dozens of women protect their businesses and dreams.

Sarah left her law firm to build a consultancy for women entrepreneurs. Within two years, she was making more than ever on her terms.

Aisha's ripple was different. She went from "just a bookkeeper" to running a strategic financial consulting firm that helped service providers scale to multiple six figures..

Tamara's ripple was built from her life as a stay-at-home mom. She turned her household management skills into an operations consulting business, helping entrepreneurs organize and breathe again.

Each started with doubt. Each took one step. And those steps created ripples far beyond their own lives.

Your First 90 Days in Aligned Action

Clarity without action is wasted potential. Here's a simple roadmap you can follow right now to turn insight into momentum and build profit with purpose.

Days 1–30: Clarity & Foundation

- ☐ Write your one-sentence offer.
- ☐ Identify three problems you solve.
- ☐ Choose one to focus on.
- ☐ Talk to three people who have that problem.

Sample calendar cue: *Block one 30-minute slot each week this month to reach out for these conversations. By the end of 30 days, you'll have real feedback instead of just guesses.*

Days 31–60: Refinement & Growth

- ☐ Create and test your minimum viable offer.
- ☐ Gather feedback and refine.
- ☐ Share your story publicly.

Sample calendar cue: *Mark one "Feedback Friday" on your calendar to pause, review, and adjust your offer before stepping into the next week.*

Days 61–90: Scale & Sustainability

- ☐ Build simple systems for delivery and onboarding.
- ☐ Explore partnerships.
- ☐ Plan your next iteration.

Sample calendar cue: *Use the last week of this 90-day sprint to map the next quarter. What worked? What needs adjusting? This reflection ensures your growth stays aligned.*

Playing the Long Game

Success isn't built in one season. It's built on the steady decision to show up, grow through challenges, and keep aligning your business with the life you want most.

Eight years ago, in 2017, I was walking around with this idea stuck in my head. An idea that followed me everywhere, whispered to me in moments of chaos, and demanded my attention.

By year 2 (2019), life forced me to rebuild my business in hospital rooms, and every iteration since has been about choosing alignment over hustle.

Today, I run a multiple-six-figure business that gives me freedom, flexibility, and impact, serving more than 300 women business owners to date, many of whom have doubled or even tripled their revenue after applying my frameworks.

And I'm still iterating. My current focus is helping women business owners not just scale to $100K months, but scale with intention, building business models that protect their time, energy, and families, while elevating them into confident CEO leaders with sustainable authority.

Do I still doubt myself sometimes? Absolutely. Do I still get nervous before launches? Of course.

The difference now is that I know those feelings mean I'm growing.

Your journey will look different from mine. It will be messy and imperfect and beautiful. But it will be worth it.

The world doesn't need you perfect. It needs you to be *willing*.

So, before you close this chapter, write down one action you can take in the next 48 hours. Not next month. Not when things "settle down". Now.

Because your future self is counting on you.

Wendy Johnson

Founder of Designed To Be HER

https://www.facebook.com/raven77143
https://www.instagram.com/wendyravenjohnson/
Human Design Blueprint - https://designedtobeher.com/report
Designed To Be HER - https://designedtobeher.com/

Wendy Johnson (Raven) is the founder of Designed to Be HER™, a soul-led space for high-achieving women who look successful on the outside but feel disconnected on the inside. A Registered Nurse with a background in corporate leadership, she brings clinical insight and soulful strategy to helping women see themselves clearly—often for the first time. She uses Human Design as the most precise method to make the invisible undeniable—bridging the seen and the unseen. Wendy doesn't fix identities—she unravels the lies they were built on. Her work helps women decode their true energetic blueprint, release outdated roles and rules, and remember who they've always been. She serves as a mirror for the woman who's ready to stop asking for permission, start trusting her own voice, and reclaim her power—without performing, pleasing, or pretending. Because when you stop performing and start becoming? Prosperity isn't just possible—it's inevitable.

The Mirror That Made Prosperity Inevitable

By Wendy Johnson

"She didn't find the next level in the doing—she saw it in the mirror. It was always hers. Designed, not discovered. That's when possibility turned into prosperity."
—Wendy "Raven" Johnson

When the Mirror Didn't Lie

It didn't happen on a stage.
It didn't happen in a boardroom.
It didn't even happen in a breakdown.

It happened in front of the mirror.

Half dressed. Half present. Going through the morning motions of another day, I had trained myself to survive. (To everyone else, it looked like thrive.)

I don't even know if I was brushing my teeth, fixing my face, or just buying time before doing what I was "supposed" to do next.

The bathroom lights hummed overhead. I looked up—
And I didn't recognize the woman staring back.

She was familiar, but hollow. Eyes that looked tired. A body that felt like it belonged to someone else.

Not because she looked wrong.
But because she wasn't me.

She was a version I had performed. Perfected. Maintained.

The high-achieving woman who knew how to succeed. How to smile. How to stay small in all the right ways.

When you live out of alignment long enough, even your own reflection starts to feel like a stranger.

Tell me...

Have you had that moment yet?
Where everything looks fine—but you're not?
Where your life fits—but *you* don't?

That moment was when the mask cracked—not because I was falling apart, but because I finally stood still long enough to hear the truth whisper back.

I didn't know it then, but that was my *Mirror Moment*.

That morning—just for a second—I saw the disconnect.

The tension between who I had become and who I truly was. Between the version of me that looked successful, and the woman who felt invisible inside of it.

That's when the mirror stopped reflecting who I thought I had to be—and started revealing who I truly was.

That moment became the start of the framework I now carry: **The Mirror. The Map. The Movement.**

And then, just like that, it hit me—soft, but undeniable.

Like the low static of a frequency I used to know.
I paused.

It was not a shout, but a whisper. Quiet. Unmistakable. And it came through so clearly.

I didn't say it out loud.
But I heard it.
Clearer than anything I had let myself admit in years:

What are we doing?

Not just the meeting.
Not just the calendar.
Not just the pretending.

But *this*—

This performance of a life that looked right but felt wrong.
This version of success that asked me to abandon myself a little more each day.
This woman in the mirror—put together, productive, praised—and painfully disconnected.

It wasn't—*What am I doing?* Because it wasn't just mine.

It was the programming. The pressure. The performance.
The identity I had built by default... instead of by design.

Why do we keep betraying ourselves to belong?
Why do we call this success when we don't even recognize the woman in the mirror?

That gentle voice I heard?
It was a frequency—one I finally tuned into that day.

The truth hadn't been missing. It had been muffled.
Like a signal I could almost hear but never quite tune into.

The signs were always there.
The static was constant.
I just kept turning up the volume on everything else, hoping the noise would drown out the knowing.

But that day?

That day was the beginning of the unraveling.
The remembering.
The return.

Of *HER*.

That moment didn't come with fireworks.
It came with clarity.

And once I saw HER—once I heard that whisper—I couldn't go back.

Because that whisper? That frequency?

It was mine.
Finally turned back on.
And waiting to be turned all the way up.

 HER Reflection Prompt:
What version of yourself are you still performing to stay safe? And what truth have you muted—because you knew it would change everything?

I Was Rewarded for Who I Wasn't

Before I ever heard the whisper, I had already perfected the performance. I was exceptional at everything that was expected of me.

I didn't just know the role—I *embodied* it. The achiever. The caregiver. The one who had it together. I knew how to lead. How to serve. How to keep it all together—even when I was falling apart inside.

I knew how to read a room. Shrink my tone. Shape-shift into whoever they needed me to be. I wasn't performing for applause. I was performing for safety.

From the outside, everything looked golden. The degrees. The promotions. The praise.
The competent woman who knew what to do, when to do it, and how to make it all look effortless.

But inside? I was slipping into roles I never auditioned for—just to make it through. Smiling with my mouth while my soul clenched its fists. Wondering when someone was finally going to notice that I was tired of being "her."

Somewhere along the way, I learned that the safest thing I could be... was perfect. If I could just do more, give more, *be* more—maybe I'd finally feel like enough.

The scary part? I got really good at it.

I was the woman who could be counted on. The one they came to for answers. The one who made it look easy. The woman who kept it together. The leader who held space for everyone—except herself.

Success became my script. And I hit my marks flawlessly.

But there's a difference between *being good at something* and *being fulfilled by it.*

You can be admired and *invisible* at the same time.
You can be applauded for a life that slowly erases you.

And I was running on empty. Praise was my fuel. Perfection was my armor. I wore both like survival. And somewhere along the way, I stopped asking if any of it was actually mine.

Tell me...
Where are *you* still performing?

Where have you confused applause for alignment?

Have you ever looked at your life and thought: *This is everything I was supposed to want.*

So, why does it feel like I'm disappearing inside it?

That's when the cracks started to show—quiet, but impossible to ignore.

I know how exhausting it is to keep winning while secretly wondering if you're even playing the right game.

The truth?
You can be excellent at something but still not belong there.
You can build a life that earns standing ovations... and still feel like a stranger behind the curtain.

That was me. What looked like confidence was often compliance. What looked like clarity was control.

A particular kind of grief comes from realizing you've been praised for your performance—but not seen in your truth.

That's what the performance years felt like.
I wasn't living in alignment.
I was surviving by curation.

And the more I succeeded, the more I disappeared.

I wasn't building a life. I was maintaining a persona.

That's what no one tells you about success.

They celebrate your performance, but they don't see the woman who had to mute herself to earn the part.

But you see her—because you *are* her.

And somewhere inside you—just like inside me—there's a version of you who is no longer willing to play along. Because the version they celebrated was never the woman I came here to be.

She was my mask. My shield. My placeholder. But never my truth.

The real me? She was under the surface. Waiting. Watching.

She's not loud. She's not angry. She's just... awake.

And she's been watching you perform.
Waiting for the moment you finally turn toward her and say:

"I see you. I remember you."

It wasn't all fake. That's what made it harder to spot. The achievements were real. The ambition was real. The care was real.

But the **cost**?

The cost was *me.*

🐣 **HER Reflection Prompt:**
Where are you still performing successfully while feeling disconnected from it?

And what identity have you outgrown—yet continue to wear to be accepted?

Tiny Moves. Massive Truth

The shift didn't come with fireworks. It didn't look like reinvention.

It looked like a *subtle rebellion.*
Like saying "no"—and not explaining.
Like slowing down long enough to realize I was holding my breath in my own life.

These were the tiny, defiant moves.
Not dramatic.
Not destructive.
Just... honest.

I didn't throw my life away. I peeled back the parts that never belonged to me.

Little moments where I picked truth over performance. Alignment over approval.
Presence over perfection.

They didn't seem like much from the outside. But to me?
They were everything.

Because when you've spent years performing to stay safe, telling the truth—even just to yourself—feels radical.

And the more I listened, the clearer it became: My passion wasn't building a brand. It wasn't climbing a ladder. It wasn't strategy or structure.

It was soul.
It was remembrance.
It was HER.

Tell me the truth...
Have you felt her, too?
That flicker of a woman who doesn't want to burn it all down—but knows she can't keep pretending either?

That's not a breakdown. That's your becoming.

And when you stop silencing that flicker? That's when everything starts to change.

I wasn't trying to change my life.
I was trying to *hear my own voice underneath all the noise.*

The part of me I had edited to fit. The version of me I used to be before I started performing for approval.
The real me.

It wasn't about burning it all down. It was about letting myself be seen again—*first by me.*

One thought.

One frequency.
One possibility that refused to be silenced:

"What if being you was enough?"

That question cracked something open.
Not because I fully believed it—but because *some part of me wanted to.*

I couldn't unhear the voice.
I couldn't unsee the mirror.

That tiny spark—barely visible to the outside world—became a bonfire in my body.

Because suddenly... I remembered.

I remembered that my power wasn't in the pretending.
It wasn't in the checklist.
It wasn't in how good I was at being who they needed me to be.

My power was buried in the parts of me I had muted to survive.

And when I let that massive truth rise?
It didn't explode.

It expanded.
It breathed.
It pulsed.

And it whispered:

"You were never meant to be someone else's version of success. You were meant to be HER."

That was when possibility stopped feeling like a far-off dream... and started feeling like *mine.*

Not because I had a plan.
But because—for the first time in a long time—

I had ME.

 HER Reflection Prompt:

What have you always known but kept silencing yourself to stay safe?

And what might finally move if you trusted the truth in the stillness?

The Map: Human Design as My Strategy

The deeper I got into the truth, the louder the question became: "If I'm not all the roles I've been playing... Who am I?"

It didn't all come rushing back at once. It came in waves. It came through remembrance.

The truth I had buried under performance started resurfacing as whispers I could finally hear.

I didn't want another label. I wasn't looking for another system. I didn't need another plan.

I needed something that wouldn't tell me who to be—but reflect who I already was beneath the noise.

I needed a blueprint of HER.
A map back to myself.
A mirror to the truth I had muted to survive.

That's what Human Design became for me.
Not a label. Not a box.
A reflection.
A blueprint.
A new strategy.

A sacred reminder that my essence wasn't lost—it was buried under years of performance, pressure, and pretending.

For the first time, I saw in print what I had always felt—but never had permission to trust.

And when I started to see my energetic blueprint... everything that never made sense suddenly clicked.

The pressure I felt.
The patterns I repeated.
The permission I was always craving—
It was right there in black and white.

That was the shift. That was the remembering. That was the moment I stopped asking:
"What should I do?"
And started asking:
"What's already true for me?"

The way I speak.
The way I move.
The energy I carry.
The way I walk into a room and feel everything.
The way I hold truth in my bones before it's spoken.
The voice I kept muting because it didn't sound like theirs.
The reason I kept dimming, doubting, and deferring—

It wasn't wrong. It wasn't broken.
It was how I was designed.

And that changed everything.

Because when I saw it? When I felt it?
I remembered.

It didn't hand me an identity. It helped me remember mine.
It revealed I already had one.

That's when I stopped trying to fix myself— and started learning how to trust myself.

I remembered that my passion wasn't in the doing. It wasn't in helping women chase more success, more systems, more validation.

That's when I stopped helping women chase more strategy—and started guiding them back to the one thing they've never needed to earn:

Themselves.

Not through another formula. But through the Frequency Mirror.

Where their blueprint isn't something to decode— It's something to finally believe.

Because when a woman sees herself clearly?
She becomes unstoppable.

Tell me...

What parts of you have you labeled "too much" or "not enough," simply because no one knew how to mirror them back to you?

What if your truth was never the problem? What if it's the mirror to the map?

The permission you've been waiting for?
It's already yours.

You don't need to hustle for it. You just need to remember it.

Not by becoming someone new—but by becoming who you were **before the world told you who to be.**

That's why I say Human Design is my strategy.

It didn't give me permission. It showed me I never needed to ask for it.

Because when you know how you're designed, you stop forcing what's not aligned.

You stop chasing strategies that override your truth.
You stop apologizing for what makes you powerful.

And you start listening to the frequency that's always been there...

Waiting to be turned back up.

 **HER Reflection Prompt:**

What part of yourself have you silenced or misunderstood—
because the world didn't know how to mirror it back to you?
And what would it feel like to finally believe what's already been
true all along—without needing to justify it?

The Movement: I Didn't Build It—I Became It

Once I stopped performing...
Once I started remembering...
Once I tuned into the truth of who I was—there was no going back.

But I didn't start a business. I didn't launch a brand. I didn't map
out a funnel.

I followed a frequency.
And for the first time—that was enough.

From quiet, sacred moments where I chose alignment over
applause.
Where I said no to what looked good and yes to what felt right.
Where I followed my body before I followed a business plan.

I built HER the same way I remembered her—**one choice at a time.**

The choice to speak more slowly. To move with intention. To build a
brand that felt like soul work, not a performance.

There was no launch. There was no viral moment.

There was just me...

Being her.
Before anyone else could see her.

Because the becoming doesn't start when the world notices.
It starts when you do.

When you stop betraying your design just to fit into someone else's formula.
That's when HER begins to rise.

She's not the polished version. She's not the filtered one. She's not the woman you build to be liked.

She's the woman you remember.

The more I honored my truth, the more I heard it—the pulse, the knowing, the vision I hadn't been able to name until I became the woman who could carry it.

Designed to Be HER™ didn't come from strategy.
It came from stillness.
It came from seeing myself clearly—and deciding never to abandon that version of me again.

At first, I didn't even call it that. I was just speaking differently.
Serving differently.
Being different.

But the more I lived it, the clearer it became: This wasn't just about me.
This was a movement.

Tell me...

What are you building right now?
And is it being shaped by your **truth**—or your **fear**?

Because what I've learned is this:

When you stop waiting to be picked...

When you stop trying to prove your worth...
You stop building for *them*.
And you start becoming her.

That's what Designed to Be HER™ is:

Not a rebrand.
A return.

A reclamation for every woman who spent years shape-shifting to survive.
A reflection for the ones who looked successful—but felt invisible inside their own lives.
A frequency they'd forgotten how to hear—until they saw themselves in me.

I didn't set out to teach Human Design.
I set out to mirror women back to themselves.

To help them remember who they were *before* the roles. Before the rules. Before the performance.

I'm not here to help women become something new.
I'm here to help them come back to HER.

The woman who was always there—just silenced by the performance.

🖐 HER Reflection Prompt:

What are you being called to create—not from your training, but your truth?
And what would happen if you stopped trying to "build" a brand... and let your embodiment be the brand?

Alignment Is the New Currency

This wasn't the prosperity I was taught to chase.

It didn't come from the perfect strategy. Or the optimized content. Or the twenty-step plan.

I didn't arrive at prosperity through a funnel. I arrived through remembrance. Through the sacred, silent work of choosing my voice—before anyone else reflected it back.

I didn't need to build a business that looked right. I needed to build a life that *felt* right.

It came the moment I stopped performing and started becoming. The moment I stopped outsourcing my voice and started trusting it.

And when I did? The ideas landed. The offers clicked.

That's when possibility turned into prosperity.

Not just numbers—but energy.

It looked like peace in my nervous system.
Clarity in my choices.
Confidence that didn't come from credentials—but from knowing I could never lead others deeper than I was willing to go myself.

It looked like alignment, which I didn't have to earn.

I didn't "monetize my passion." I trusted it before it proved itself. Before it produced. I let it lead.

And that trust became the foundation for everything I'm building now—a body of work.
A mirror. A movement.

Because I realized clarity was already making me rich—just not the way I'd been taught to measure it.

See… the real currency isn't content.

When your inside and your outside finally match?
You don't have to push anymore. You *pull*. With your presence.

With your truth.

That's what HER became for me:

A body of work.
A living mirror.
A new standard.

Not built to impress. Built to activate.

Tell me...

What would your life look like if prosperity didn't require you to abandon yourself—but to finally embody the version of you that's been whispering all along?

Because it's not just possible. It's *inevitable.*

Once you stop performing. Once you start becoming. Once you remember who you were before the world asked you to shrink.

That's when everything changes.

Not because you tried harder.
But because you finally remembered HER.

◑ HER Reflection Prompt:
What's your version of prosperity—when no one else is watching? And what truth are you still silencing... that might just set it all in motion?

The Mirror's Facing You NOW

You've been waiting for a sign.
Maybe it's in the woman you've always been—beneath the performance, behind the roles, beyond the noise.

Because here's the truth: You don't need a new identity. You don't need to fix yourself. You don't need to prove anything before you begin.

You just need to stop trying to fit into something that was never designed for you.

Because HER—the real you—was never lost.

She was just muted.

And something in you remembered, too. Not a new version. Not a new strategy.

But the truth. *Your* truth.

You didn't just read my story—you felt yours.

You saw yourself braided through every line.

And now the mirror is facing you.

No more shrinking. No more second-guessing. No more waiting to feel "ready."

This is your mirror moment—the one you can't unsee.

The one where you finally decide:

I don't have to become someone new. I just have to become HER.

The one who remembers how to lead, love, speak, and serve... from truth, not performance.

So, let's get honest. No filter. No delay.

If you're still here, I know why.

Because something in you remembered, too.

Not a strategy. Not a role.

But yourself.

HER Possibility to Prosperity Activation

You don't need to earn your clarity.

You don't need to wait for permission to take up space, speak your truth, or change your entire life.

You've always known. You've just been conditioned to forget.

But HER?

She's still here. Beneath the roles. Behind the performance.

She's not waiting for the right time. She's waiting for you.

So, stop dimming.
Stop performing.
Stop waiting to feel "ready."

Turn your truth all the way up.
Become the woman you were always designed to be.

Because when you stop muting, shrinking, second-guessing, pleasing, perfecting...
That's when you become HER.
And *that's* when everything changes.

This isn't the end. This is remembering.
This is what it means to go from possibility... to prosperity.

Not by becoming someone else.
But by becoming HER.

You don't need to change everything overnight.
You just need to say *yes* to the version of you who already knows.

🥚 HER Activation: Your First Move

You're not here to read. You're here to remember.

This is your mirror moment. Now it's time to move.

1. Look in the Mirror—Again.
Ask:
- Who have I been performing as?
- Who am I becoming?

Write it all down—raw, unfiltered, real. Let it pour out.

2. Tune Into the Frequency.
Five minutes.
Hand on heart. Eyes closed.

Ask:

- What does my next level *feel* like?

Let your body speak before your mind tries to fix the answer.

3. Read the Map.

Download your Frequency Mirror Report →
https://humandesignforher.com/

This isn't another tool.
It's your design. Your blueprint.
The map that reflects your power to you.
Don't print it and forget it—let it change how you lead.

4. Take the Tiny Move.

HER doesn't wait for permission.
She moves—now.
Raise the price. Speak the truth. Post the message. Pause the plan.
Whatever "tiny" looks like, do it today.
Because tiny moves create massive shifts.

5. Let the Mirror Speak Back.

This movement now lives in your voice.
Tag [@designedtobeher] or use #BecomingHER—
So I can reflect HER right back to you.

🪁 The Mirror. The Map. The Movement.

The Mirror — the moment you saw yourself clearly. No filters. No performance. Just presence.

The Map — your Human Design blueprint. Not a chart—a reflection. The design you've always carried—now decoded.

The Movement — the embodiment of your truth. In business. In life. In leadership.

This is the beginning of a new frequency—yours.
The woman you were always designed to be.

And when you do that?
The shift is real.
The energy is different.
The momentum is magnetic.

Because when you stop performing and start becoming?

Prosperity isn't just possible. It's inevitable.

XOXO

Raven

Dr. Araba Afenyi-Annan

Founder of Hooray 4 Healing
Certified Spiritual Counselor and
Transformational Parenting Mentor

linkedin.com/in/araba-afenyi-annan-48218510
https://www.facebook.com/profile.php?id=61556671719462
instagram.com/Hooray4Healing
https://www.hooray4healing.com
https://link.pfnls.com/widget/bookings/masterfulempowered

Dr. Araba Afenyi-Annan, MD MPH is a retired physician, educator, and former expert in sickle cell disease. When a life-changing injury cut her brilliant medical career short and left her mind and body ravaged by severe debilitating pain and chronic illness, her two young children became her life-saving blessings. Fueled by her love for them and inspired by their unconditional love for her, she found herself on a profound healing journey. Dr. Araba combines her training as a spiritual counselor, small group facilitator, previous experience as a dynamic speaker and leader, with her expanded capacity to hold compassionate, sacred space for her clients, born from more than a decade of living with chronic pain. As a transformational parenting mentor working with moms of faith with school aged children and spiritually mature mothers and grandmothers, Dr. Araba is redefining parenting as a pathway for transformation, generational healing, and elevating human consciousness.

Finding Home:
When Life's Detour Becomes the Path

By Dr. Araba Afenyi-Annan

"You were always different. Even in high school, you were on a different level from the rest of us."

It was a gray, wet day that prevented even a glimpse of the sun from being seen. The sky had been replaced by a blanket of woolly white as far as the eye could see. Although it wasn't actually cold, I shivered as the familiar sensation of cold moved through me. I smiled. It always showed up before a profound realization.

Tucked away in the back corner of the bustling new French pastry shop, La Patisserie, I clutched my cup of hot, fragrant tea with both hands and turned my attention back to you. I leaned forward, listening intently, and searched your words for some recognition, a glimmer of remembering the person you were talking about. We had gone to high school together, but lost touch a few years into college. Decades later, we were reunited through the magic of Facebook. My parents had moved to a different state by the time I had graduated from medical school, so I had not seen our high school in years. Yet, here I was sitting across the street from it, talking to my old lab partner, Michael.

"You had your whole life mapped out," he said. *"You knew what you wanted to do and how you were going to get there. No one doubted that you were going to be a doctor. You were supersmart...the newspaper articles, the plaque and your picture on the wall, the awards and achievements. For goodness sakes, you used to read the encyclopedia for fun!"*

We both chuckled, before he continued.

"Most of our high school class just wanted to graduate and go to college, to get a good job, basically to do better than our parents, and maybe after

that, get married and have kids. But not you, you wanted more. You wanted to change the world. No, you were determined to change the world," he said with a wry smile, followed by a full-bodied laugh.

"Very few people suspect the strength of will that lives within your petite frame, underneath the sweet, soft voice. I think you underestimate what you are capable of and always have. I mean think about it. Even though you aren't practicing medicine, your focus is still on helping people heal. It's funny. In a way, you have come full circle, right?"

"I mean, I'm sure you were a great doctor, but the work you do now? You light up from the inside out. Your energy, your passion, and the wisdom you share? It seems like you were born for this, to be a healer. Perhaps this was where you were always meant to end up?"

I listened, fascinated by his perception of who I had been four decades ago and how that connected to who I was now. Somehow, he really knew me, even though I did not remember much about being that high school student. How interesting to discover that I was returning to being the person I once was, but had forgotten being. How confusing. Or perhaps not...*A Course in Miracles (ACIM)* tells us that we are all walking a journey we have already walked and completed. The end is certain. God is inevitable, for God is all there is. This is the affirmation and confirmation that we all make it, being inextricably linked to one another.

In my mind, that young lady ceased to exist a lifetime ago. She was a victim of trauma, medical training, and of life in the "real world." From the outside looking in, that young girl became a woman determined to win, one who would not let anyone or anything stand in her way. With each defeat, she seemed to come back stronger and tougher, until she didn't. Until she couldn't. No matter how hard she worked, she could not reinvent herself. There was no mask she could hide behind or version to become that would make her more lovable, respected, or valued. Oh, she had tried for years to operate as she had always done, only to find that every small gain came with a spectacular crash and burn, each time reaching new depths of hell.

It had never occurred to me that I was still in the business of healing. I would have to explore that further at a later time. My medical career had been unexpectedly and abruptly cut short. I now lived with a chronic pain syndrome from herniated discs and a lumbar radiculopathy. I pushed away the memories that threatened to catapult me back to the moment my life changed forever. Instead, I focused on being fully present here. *Thank goodness for our breath!* I silently offered up my gratitude for this perfect anchor to the present. It is not possible to breathe in the past, nor in the future, only in the present moment. After taking several long exhales coupled with deep inhales, I spoke.

"I am not a healer." I went on to explain, *"At least that is not the way I think about it. You see, I do not heal other people. The only person that I have the power to heal is myself. I learned that during my training to become a certified spiritual counselor and three years working for the Ministry where I trained. I learned that my healing is not just for me; it is shared with everyone. I heal as I allow myself to be a conduit for healing. My clients heal themselves."*

It was clear that he did not quite understand or believe my words, so I continued.

"I hold the Light and vibration of Truth for them, just as it was held for me. I invite them to join me in a sacred space, never forgetting it is an honor to receive another person's trust to walk with them on their path. Before you ask, a sacred space is a place, but more importantly, it's a state of being where you feel safe enough to meet yourself honestly. And even if there is fear, you have the courage to explore what is there. You understand that you do not walk this life alone, despite what it might feel like; you are seen, heard, and valued. It's a place where you discover that the judgment and condemnation you are so sure you'll receive is actually your own. Love,

forgiveness, compassion, acceptance...these are the practices and gifts that act as catalysts for healing."

Later that day, at home, alone, I let the memories come flooding in...

It was an ordinary day in August when my life was torn apart. I awoke to find my 2-year-old son lethargic. This was the child who couldn't sit still. He was an early riser, typically full of life and energy from the moment he woke up until he literally collapsed at night. I knew immediately that he was sick. The thermometer reading confirmed my suspicions. With dread, I went to my daughter's room to find her sleeping, which was typical, but she was also not feeling well. My husband had already left for work. I was supposed to drop the kids off at daycare before heading to the hospital. *No daycare today,* I thought, and possibly tomorrow, depending on whether their fevers broke.

I had just come off of a week of service and a weekend on call, so I knew I had the flexibility to take a day off. I marveled that I had left my pager in my office. I had gotten to a place where I could comfortably leave my pager at work when I wasn't the attending physician. For so long, whether I was "on service" or not, I felt responsible for making myself available at all times, just in case someone, my staff or another physician, might need my help. Things had recently changed, though. When I returned back to work after 15 weeks of maternity leave after the birth of our second child, my priorities had shifted. My patients, my research, teaching, publishing–those things were no longer at the top of my mind. It was my family. I lived for the moment when I picked the kids up from daycare, and they ran excitedly to me with big hugs and joy. My joy matched theirs; it felt like a part of me was missing when they were not with me. My days revolved around the minutes until I could be with them again.

After letting work know that I was taking a sick day, I turned my attention to making sure everybody was fed and had their own individual time with mom reading and snuggling. I also got the chance to nap when they did. I was always tired. I was a mom after all. Then after that, a physician who was on call every 3rd night or so. I had multiple administrative roles and a National Institutes of Health (NIH) grant working with my colleagues at the other prestigious institution "down the street". Additionally, I had a couple of papers to prepare for publication and a newly appointed seat at the table of the NIH expert panel, which reviews and updates the practice guidelines for patients with sickle cell disease. I was the first pathologist and transfusion medicine physician to have ever been a part of this. Hematologists were considered the experts on sickle cell management but my experience and research with these patients, combined with my blood donation research, provided a unique perspective on the needs of this patient population, adverse consequences, and resource management. My reverie was cut short as I heard my daughter and then my son call for me.

After a light supper, both kids were feeling better and I got them into the tub. I filled the tub with their favorite toys and lots of bubble bath, giving them some time to play, while also getting them ready for bed by the time my husband got home from work, so we could split the bedtime duties. I reached down and picked up my light, petite 4-year-old daughter out of the tub and started getting her dry. Then, I picked up my 2-year-old son. His favorite place was in my arms, and I loved carrying him. He was a solid kid, weighing nearly the same as my daughter. As I did, something seemed to tear in my body. I felt a searing pain move through my back and barely got him safely to the ground.

My eyes widened, and my breath unsteady, I started to pray as I finished drying him off. *Please Lord, please let me not scare the children.* The pain was unlike anything I had felt before. My entire back felt on fire. *Please Lord, please let my husband get home!* As I finished thinking those words, there he was.

"How is everyone doing?" he asked with a smile. He saw my face, clearly in distress, but I silently shook my head to let him know I did not want the kids to know.

"Let's let mom get a break since she has taken care of you all day. It's my turn," he said, tickling them. They laughed and squealed with delight and went to get their pajamas on. Meanwhile, I crawled slowly to our bedroom through a mix of tears and prayers. *Lord, help me.* I managed to make it to our bedroom, to the bed. I only vaguely remember my husband coming in later, very concerned, wondering what was wrong, and asking if there was anything he could do to help.

"It's my back. It feels like it is broken." Staying as still as I could, I prayed the meds would help and sleep would overtake me quickly. I fell into a fitful rest.

The next day, I was still hurting and unable to move very well. My husband was even more concerned, but I waved it off saying, *"I think it will get better with some ibuprofen and rest. Don't worry."* Three days later, after trying rubs and creams, heating pads, and ibuprofen, I was only minimally better and called my doctor. I was prescribed Valium as a muscle relaxant, and it worked wonders. For the first time in days, I had some relief. However, I was clearly under the influence and could not work while taking this medicine. Three weeks later, I went back to work. My condition was clearly more than a strain, but no one quite knew what it was.

It was soon obvious that I was unable to work. I could not open the door to get into the hospital without setting my back off into uncontrollable, painful spasms. I could not get into my office without assistance. I was irritable and short-tempered. During rounds, all I could think about was going to my office to lie down. I was undergoing testing and doing physical therapy, during the day, while at the hospital. Again, that was short-lived. I could not get into my car because I was so locked up with spasms. I tried injections while my doctors continued to try to understand what had happened, but no one could account for the degree of pain and disability I had. My diagnoses ranged from fibromyalgia, slipped disc with involvement of the nerve root, somatic disorder, depression, lupus, etc. All I knew was that I had medical appointments 2-3 times a week. I could not drive, so I had to arrange my own transportation.

My master's degree in public health failed to provide an adequate education on what it was actually like to be a chronic user of medical services. How things always fell through the cracks and it was always the patient's responsibility. Suddenly, I remembered the experiences of my sickle cell patients. I was now in their seat. I quickly learned that doctors and clinics did not want to see you if there was any chance you might be filing workers' comp or disability. I remember the day I stopped trusting my doctor, who was also a colleague. She suggested that my back pain was not getting better because of depression and told me very clearly that she didn't "do disability."

After seeing a psychiatrist, who ruled out depression, I began to seek other care. Another doctor in the group specialized in sports medicine, orthopedics, and family medicine. He saw my suffering and suggested I consider a longer period of leave. I resisted. Then my boss pulled me aside one day and told me that the best thing I could do was go on medical leave, both for the sake of the service and for my own well-being. Crying, I called my doctor and told him "Yes, let's start the process." As I painfully hobbled to my car, I remember thinking how could I be here in this place when four months ago I was at the peak of life. I was only 39 years old. I wondered what would happen.

What happened? Medical leave turned into short-term disability. Short-term disability turned into retirement and long-term disability. I never went back to work. I never got to say goodbye. Nine months later, my contract was not renewed. I was terminated. One year after I went on medical leave, my entire office was packed up and delivered to my home. At the time, I was too sick and managing medical appointments, mental health appointments, surgeons, physical medicine and rehabilitation, the pain clinic and many more while fighting with the insurance company, which denied my claim. I was 40 years old, retired, on disability, forced to apply for social security, married and raising children. Then, I had my first three surgeries within four months. And that fundamentally changed me. I lost the will to live.

There comes a time when you have to grapple with the fact that this is not going to end, never going to get better. Something switches off in your soul when you realize things will not return "back to normal," and all that is left is to endure–and pray it would not be long. I prayed. Others prayed. But there was no more fight in me. I had nothing left to continue to fight the pain. Instead, I tried being awake and aware as little as possible. Sleep was the only place I could gain a temporary respite from hell. So I began to drink alcohol daily with all of my meds – short-acting and long-acting narcotics, Valium, muscle relaxants, ibuprofen, depression medication, Ativan for panic attacks, sleep medication and more; yet somehow, I didn't die.

One night, it nearly became too much. My husband was out of town at a conference and I was drowning in the sea of pain, struggling to even breathe. All I could think about was making the pain stop. My beautiful sister stayed on the phone with me all night long while I cried and tried desperately not to act on this burning desire. Then she said words I will never forget. At the time, they barely entered into my awareness, but later they would help shape my world. She said, *"Maybe your ministry is exactly where you are."* What did that even mean? I had lost everything and was losing my marriage on top of it. My husband and I had stopped going to marital counseling after realizing that living in survival mode year after year had created a gulf between us that we could not bridge. The only thing that I could think of that was worse than my existence was to leave horror and trauma as my legacy for my children.

Then, I started a new type of intensive therapy, dialectical behavior therapy (DBT) and became armed with new life skills, tools, and perspective. As I re-learned mindfulness practices, I gained insights into my emotions and how to regulate them. I also learned tools to navigate my relationships, and practical actions I could take when in distress. I eagerly practiced all of these and wanted to learn more. I couldn't understand why no one had taught me these basic skills to navigate life. It seemed to me that these were critical skills that people needed to avoid getting into desperate straits, not skills that were used and taught when they were already there. It made no sense to me.

I began teaching my children the things I was learning. I stopped taking on their emotions as my own and realized there was nothing to fix. I learned to ask for what I wanted, to negotiate what was most important in my interactions with others, whether it was with my family, my husband, or strangers. I stopped falling apart, overcome by grief, every time I walked into the hospital for yet another procedure or surgery. I was introduced to the term radical acceptance. I started having agency. I devoted myself to being the very best mother I could be, to establish the type of bond with my children that even if I weren't physically available, they would not hesitate to trust me.

Being a mother saved my life. People think I am exaggerating when I say this, but I mean this literally, without an ounce of hyperbole. My children became the only people who did not look at me with pity and sadness for all that I had lost. Every adult in my life, while well-meaning, saw me as broken, which in turn reminded me of all I once was, and magnified my brokenness in my mind. For my beautiful babies, I was *Mom,* a safe place to be, talk, and express love. I gave them my full attention and began to know their true essence. I allowed them to express their feelings, whatever they were, but always in a respectful manner. This led me to the first of many profound realizations.

One day, my six-year-old daughter said, *"Mommy, I don't like it when you say that."*

"Say what, honey?" I asked, genuinely puzzled.

"What is wrong with you?" she replied. *"It sounds mean and hurts my feelings."*

Wow. That stopped me in my tracks. I had been asked this question my entire life. In fact, I would ask myself the question whenever I made a mistake. I realized the impact of repeatedly asking this question. It planted a seed that something was inherently wrong with a person. I stopped asking this question. I stopped trying to fix their issues and instead empowered them to know their own power. They lit up every space they entered, whether it was in church, school, gymnastics, or the playground. Love is a light that shines in us all. My children reflected my wholeness and light back to me, until I could hold it myself.

There was a time when I didn't really want to have children and definitely thought being a stay-at-home mother was beyond me. I didn't want them to know the pain I carried within myself. The pain no one saw or heard. The pain in my chest, as if my heart was burning a hole inside of me. The pain I could not explain. I told myself all I had were reasons to feel grateful. I had everything a young person could possibly want. I had a family that loved me. I had every advantage and opportunity. Although I told myself that there was nothing wrong, underneath, I knew there was something very wrong. I did not have words for it, nor anyone to talk to about it. Over time, even I forgot about that pain. I had stuffed it so far down beneath my studies and exams, joining a sorority, disappointment and shame, falling in love, getting married, buying a home, practicing medicine, chairing another committee, another title, another fellowship, our first child, our second child, and more. But my body never forgot. It simply held each hurt until it no longer could.

At the time, I knew nothing about the work of Dr. Bessel von De Kolk, a psychiatrist whose work with traumatic stress led to the book, *The Body Keeps Score: Brain, Mind, and Body in the Healing of Trauma*. This book was published several years after my injury but my own explorations were driven by a deep need to understand what had happened to me and how do I continue to live with this could I live with this. All I knew was that it felt like God had put a stop sign in front of me saying, "Go straight to jail. Do not pass go." I became confined within the jail of my body, and pain became the inescapable prison. The prison cell was a measure of how much I could accomplish in a day before I would collapse. The prison bars others could not see made me undependable, unsure of myself, and feel like a constant failure. It made me different, even if other people outside of my family couldn't see these bars. They didn't see or feel the pain that screamed in my body and in my head all day long. They could not appreciate what it took to stand upright or breathe deeply, let alone shower, dress, or hold that tidal wave at bay to have moments with others and try to live a semblance of life.

There is a saying that everything is a blessing or a lesson. I have come to know instead that there is a blessing in every lesson. That might not sound like a big shift, but it is and it was. For so long, I begged God to show me, tell me what I was to do, so that I might finally rest. I would get bits and pieces over time. Sentences like, "*Share your vision*," would be written in my journal, followed by multiple question marks. *Share what??* Bits of poetry and my past kept showing up until I walked through it all, learning what I could not see before.

One day, a Bible verse came to me. I opened my bible app every morning to read the verse of the day, but on this day, I felt the words were being spoken to me personally.

" 'For I know the plans I have for you,' declares the LORD, 'plans to prosper you and not to harm you, plans to give you hope and a future.

Then you will call on me and come and pray to me, and I will listen to you. You will seek me and find me when you seek me with all your heart.' " (Jeremiah 29: 11-14, NIVUK)

And in those words, I found comfort. The seeking stopped for I was reassured. The fear didn't stop, but my faith and courage grew — giving me the strength to look deeply within, to transform, to use my perseverance and tenacity for personal and spiritual transformation. And the peace of God would come to me in quiet moments, and I would rest in that. It gave me the strength to stop settling for being a duty and responsibility. It provided the courage to keep going in many more moments of struggle, to jump off what seemed like cliffs of insanity and trust that I would be caught. And I was.

Then, *A Course In Miracles (ACIM)* came into my life. It gave me a purpose and a function that I could do even in a broken body. It led me to a global online community that was committed to actually living the principles of ACIM. This loving community supported me through another major surgery where I had to learn how to walk again. It was a place I could show up as I was and learn to stop hiding. I learned a different way to pray and be with God. I learned to hold space for healing and watched miracles unfold in my life, one after another. I was here to be truly helpful, and my healing was intertwined with my willingness to be a conduit of healing.

A Course In Miracles urges us to:

"Teach only Love, for that is what you are." (T-6.I.13:2)

These words have been ingrained in me and help to direct my life. When we are loving, we feel lovable and loved. It is not enough to go to church, say the words, then live in a way that is incompatible with love. I strive to have my words, thoughts, actions aligned. I choose to be a Teacher of God.

I have learned so much from many people, but my children have been my greatest teachers. I have watched them develop into mature young people, confident in who they are, and able to navigate the world with ease. They are high achieving, self-regulated and self-motivated. I honor their journey knowing we are in a sacred partnership, learning from each other. I feel blessed and honored to be their mother.

I believe that my children were given to me to help me recognize all the places and spaces where false beliefs, judgments, and trapped emotions existed. I learned to have compassion for myself through them. I learned that when you go through life at 80mph, you miss a lot of things, especially important nuances. I understand that the point of life is to live the love that we are.

Our children are our future, but not in the way that most people think. Our children help us remember who we are meant to be. When my son chose me as his Hero for his 6th grade English project, I was so honored that I nearly cried. He wrote, *the three words that best describe "My Hero" are resilience, understanding, and courage.* He saw me through the eyes of Love. While we teach our children our understanding of the world, they show us the multitude of opportunities we have been given to heal ourselves, and in doing so, to heal our families.

I believe that "home" is the most powerful place to make change a reality. We must stop passing on from generation to generation beliefs and patterns that take up so much time, space and energy, that people spend half of their lives trying to repair. They say, "the hand that rocks the cradle is the hand that rules the world." But I believe the hand that rocks the cradle is the hand that shapes (not rules) the world. My work with mothers, children, and families has shown me that this is a powerful way to change the world. I envision us evolving human consciousness, freeing up our life force for good, and ushering in a new age of prosperity for all.

It is my mission to bring this forward, the mission I was given. I found my path to healing in my own home. I am honored to support mothers who also choose to walk this path. I have seen the impact of mothers who have gotten support and know wholeheartedly that our world will infinitely improve once we choose to parent differently.

Micheal asked, *"Does anyone ever ask you how you went from being a logical, rational person who doesn't believe in anything but science, to where you are now?*

"I have always believed in God, and now there is science to support what wisdom traditions have always taught," I responded. "But to answer your question – yes, I have been asked that before. When asked, I smile and say,

'Let's look at it. I would love for you to walk my journey with me. I hope it inspires you and lets you know that you are not alone, no matter what it feels like. There is a purpose to your life. Your purpose, it is not the thing you do; it is the thing you are.''

Amy Mandelj

A Tinchy Bit of Sparkle, A&T Office Admin Solutions and Amy Mandelj Growth and Empowerment Services
CEO, Tech VA, Coach/Mentor, Crystal Seller and Author

https://www.linkedin.com/in/amy-mandelj-1b3806b6/
https://www.facebook.com/amandelj
https://www.instagram.com/amymandelj/
https://www.atofficeadminsolutions.co.uk
https://www.atinchybitofsparkle.co.uk

I'm Amy Mandelj, an entrepreneur, Tech VA, coach, mentor, and advocate for empowerment and resilience. I founded A&T Office Admin Solutions to provide tailored virtual assistance, website design, and business support services, helping individuals and organisations achieve their goals. My coaching business – Amy Mandelj Growth & Empowerment Services is rooted in a passion for transformation, offering personalised accountability, business planning, leadership development, and productivity-enhancing body doubling sessions. As a single parent and neurodiverse individual, I bring a unique perspective to my work, inspiring others to embrace their strengths and overcome challenges. I'm also the co-creator of A Tinchy Bit of Sparkle, a business focused on promoting positivity and mindfulness through crystals. My journey, shaped by creativity and determination, has taught me the power of resilience and community. Through my businesses, I aim to empower others to thrive, turn their dreams into reality, and navigate life's challenges with confidence and purpose.

From Sparkle to Self-Belief: Building a Legacy of Light

By Amy Mandelj

A Whisper of Possibility

There was a time when I believed I had nothing left to give.

I was overwhelmed. Exhausted. Lost in a world that didn't feel built for me. I was juggling motherhood, chronic illness, neurodivergence and a constant undercurrent of guilt that whispered I wasn't enough. The kind of guilt that clings to you like fog. The kind that makes you question whether anything you do will ever be good enough.

I spent years putting everyone else first. Holding it all together for other people while silently falling apart. I was doing my best to survive, but I had forgotten how to dream. I had forgotten what it felt like to believe in myself. Somewhere along the way, I had accepted that burnout, people-pleasing and emotional exhaustion were just the cost of trying.

And yet, somewhere beneath the noise, a tiny voice whispered something different. Not loud. Not certain. Just... possible.

I didn't know what it would become at the time. I just knew I couldn't stay stuck in the version of myself that constantly questioned her worth. So, I did the only thing I could. I started small. With a crystal. With a jar. With an affirmation that simply said, *"I am enough."*

That simple phrase started to change everything.

Not all at once. Not with fireworks or overnight success. But in slow, steady ripples. Those ripples became waves. Those waves became something I never thought I could create. A business built with meaning. With sparkle. With legacy. A business born not just from survival but from hope. One that carried the fingerprints of my son and the truth of who I really was.

This is the story of how A Tinchy Bit of Sparkle lit a path not just for me but for others, how the smallest glimmer of belief can grow into something extraordinary, how choosing possibility, even when you're scared, is the first step toward prosperity.

Tyler's Spark – The Unexpected Beginning

I've told the story of how A Tinchy Bit of Sparkle began before. How a simple, heartfelt idea from my son Tyler turned into affirmation jars that slowly evolved into a business. But what I haven't shared, until now, is the deeper layer. The internal shift that happened not just around me, but *within* me.

Because his spark didn't just light a path for a business, it lit a path back to myself.

At the time, I was surviving. Getting by. I had moments of hope, sure, but they were scattered between exhaustion and uncertainty. I was navigating motherhood, chronic illness and the unpredictable emotions that come with anxiety and neurodivergence. I felt disconnected from joy, from trust and from any real sense of purpose.

Tyler's suggestion to put kind words with crystals was innocent and beautiful. But more than that, it held up a mirror. He offered me a message I didn't know I needed to hear. That healing doesn't have to be complicated. That belief can start with something small. That there's power in positivity, even when everything feels heavy.

The first time someone asked to buy one of our jars, I felt the tug of something unfamiliar. Possibility. I had spent so long doubting my own worth, I wasn't sure what to do with the idea that something I created could actually help someone else. That I could be someone people turned to for light, guidance and healing. I had always thought that was for "other people" – the ones who had it all together.

But what if it wasn't?

What if being a little bit broken was actually what made me the right person to create something like this?

The jars themselves were only part of the story. The real transformation began when I started believing the affirmations I was writing. I didn't just sell *"I am enough"* to others – I needed it for myself. I held those words like a lifeline. Some days, I would repeat them aloud just to drown out the voice in my head telling me I was a failure. Over time, the voice didn't disappear, but it softened. I started to choose the kinder voice more often.

Around then, I realised something that still sits with me today – maybe the power in these affirmations wasn't just about the words. Maybe it was about being willing to try again. To believe again. To *hope* again.

And slowly, as I repeated the words I was sharing with others, I began to see a version of myself I hadn't met before. A woman who wasn't just trying to survive but beginning to rise. A woman who could build something from nothing, even when her confidence was cracked around the edges.

I started to share more openly. I stopped pretending I had everything figured out. Instead, I leaned into authenticity. I let people see the mess and the magic side by side. The response was more powerful than I expected. People didn't want perfection. They wanted permission. To be themselves. To feel things. To grow at their own pace.

That was the moment it shifted. When I realised I wasn't just selling jars or crystals. I was building connections. I was creating tiny tools for healing, and each one carried a little bit of my journey inside it. Each one was proof that you could start from uncertainty and still build something beautiful.

Once I allowed myself to imagine that this could be more than a side project, things started to shift. I explored crystal meanings more deeply. I studied affirmations and spiritual practices. I began curating not just products, but experiences. From moon rituals to guided journaling and energy work, everything I created came from a place of wanting to empower others to feel the belief I was starting to feel in myself.

That spark Tyler gave me didn't just ignite a business. It woke up the part of me that had been buried under years of doubt. The part that always wanted to help others feel seen, heard and held. The part that remembered how to dream again.

That spark reminded me that I didn't have to be completely healed to help others. I just had to be willing to start. I didn't need to be an expert or have a perfect plan. I just had to bring my truth, my intention and my heart.

And that, truly, was the beginning.

Affirmations That Saved Me

When I started writing affirmations, I wasn't doing it to be inspirational. I was doing it because I was falling apart. Because my self-worth was in pieces. Because something had to change.

I needed a new voice in my head.

The old one had been there for years. The voice that told me I wasn't working hard enough. That I was letting people down. That I was too emotional. Too tired. Too much. Or not enough of the right things. It didn't matter how many kind words came from other people – that internal voice always found a way to twist them into something I couldn't trust.

So, I started writing affirmations because it felt like something I could control. When everything else was uncertain, I could at least choose a sentence. Something simple. Something gentle. Something I could hold onto when the rest of the day felt impossible.

The first one I wrote for myself was *"I am enough."* Just those three words. It felt like a lie at first. I'd write it down and instantly think of all the ways I wasn't. All the things I hadn't done. All the times I'd snapped or cancelled or avoided something out of anxiety or pain.

But I kept writing it. Over and over. I stuck it on post-its around the house. I whispered it to myself when I didn't want to get out of bed. I repeated it in the car before meetings or school runs or social events that triggered all my insecurities. And slowly, something started to shift. Not everything. Not all at once. But enough.

Enough to try. Enough to speak up. Enough to send that post. Enough to press "go live." Enough to launch the next product, message the next potential stockist, say yes to the next opportunity. The more I wrote *"I am enough,"* the more I started to believe it. The more I believed it, the more I started acting like it.

Affirmations became my anchor. Not just for my emotions, but for my identity. They reminded me of the version of myself I was working towards – the one who believed she was capable. The one who showed up even when she was scared. The one who didn't need to be perfect to be powerful.

One of the most powerful affirmations I ever used – and still do – is *"I can and I will."* It's so simple, but it cuts through all the noise in my head. It doesn't ask for permission. It doesn't wait to be ready. It just claims it.

That phrase helped me start my second business. It helped me show up on camera when I hated how I looked. It helped me take coaching calls through flare-ups, write through brain fog and build my website while dealing with mum guilt, fatigue and fear. It also helped me say no when I needed to protect my energies and yes when something scared me but felt right deep down. *"I can and I will"* reminded me that I didn't need to have it all figured out. I just needed to trust myself enough to take one step. Then, another. Then, another.

I started building these affirmations into everything I did. They weren't just words anymore – they were energy. They became part of my brand. Part of my products. Part of my story. I created jars, guides, social posts and journal prompts that shared these messages because I knew there were other women out there who needed to hear them, too.

And I didn't want to be the expert who told them what to do. I wanted to be the voice that said, "I've been where you are. And here's what helped me. Maybe it'll help you, too."

That's the heart of everything I create. Not perfection. Not pressure. Just possibility.

I think that's why affirmations work. Because they don't ask you to be someone you're not, they just give you a new thought to try on. And sometimes, that's all it takes to create space. Space for healing. Space for clarity. Space for growth.

Of course, there are still days when I fall into old patterns. Days when I question myself. Days when the inner critic speaks louder than the affirmations. But I come back to them anyway because they've never failed me. Because they meet me where I am. And because they remind me that progress doesn't always look loud or bold. Sometimes, it looks like saying, *"I am enough,"* even when you're crying on the kitchen floor.

What I've learned through all of this is that affirmations aren't just self-help tools. They're survival tools. They're business tools. They're belief systems in the making. They've helped me show up for my son, for my clients, and most importantly, for myself.

They helped me rebuild my self-worth in a world that often told me I was broken. They helped me shape a business around intention, not just income. They helped me show others that even in the middle of messiness, they are still worthy. Still powerful. Still *enough*.

And maybe, more than anything, affirmations helped me remember who I was before the world made me forget.

Crystals, Clients, and Confidence – Growing the Business with Purpose

When I started A Tinchy Bit of Sparkle, I didn't have a business plan. I had a kitchen table, a few affirmation ideas and a small collection of crystals. I didn't know what I was doing, but I knew how I wanted people to feel.

I wanted them to feel held. Seen. Uplifted. Connected to something bigger than the day-to-day stress or self-doubt they carried.

That vision guided every decision I made in those early stages. I didn't look at trends or follow strategies that didn't feel good. I trusted my instincts. I created the things I needed. The things I wished had been there for me when I was in the darkest parts of my journey.

It started with affirmation jars, but soon it grew into something much deeper. I found myself drawn to the energy and history of crystals. Each one carried its own story. Its own healing properties. Its own message. The more I worked with them, the more I realised how powerful they could be as tools for emotional wellbeing and self-awareness.

I didn't just want to sell "pretty stones." I wanted every piece to have a purpose. Whether it was a grounding tower for someone with anxiety, a rose quartz bracelet to support someone healing from heartbreak, or a full moon ritual set to help someone release what was no longer serving them – everything I offered was infused with meaning.

I researched. I tested. I created simple guides and rituals for people who were new to crystals and spiritual tools. I didn't want anyone to feel intimidated or "not spiritual enough" to get involved. I wanted it to feel accessible, gentle and empowering. I spoke the way I speak. I made the content neurodivergent-friendly. Bite-sized. Visual. Straight to the point.

As I grew, I listened to my audience. Every message, every review, every question helped shape the next step. People weren't just buying products. They were buying hope. Reassurance. Encouragement. They were looking for tools to help them feel better and stronger. That's a responsibility I never took lightly.

There were plenty of times I could have scaled quicker or taken shortcuts. But I never wanted growth at the cost of integrity. If a supplier didn't feel right, I didn't use them. If a product didn't hold the energy I wanted, I didn't sell it. If I couldn't package something with care and intention, I paused until I could.

I reinvested with purpose. I improved packaging to feel more like an experience. I introduced more ethically sourced pieces. I added oracle decks, moon phase guides, carved shapes and little pocket stones for kids or beginners. I started to design ranges around emotions – like calm, clarity, or confidence – so that customers didn't need to know the names of every crystal. They could shop based on how they wanted to feel.

There were lessons, of course. Times I got it wrong. Times I overgave or undercharged. Times I questioned everything because sales dipped or algorithms changed or illness flared up, and I couldn't keep up with everything. But even in those moments, the thing that kept me going was knowing the *why* behind it all.

I wasn't just building a shop. I was building a space.

A space for people to breathe. A space for people to believe in something again. A space where spirituality wasn't about rules or perfection – it was about self-discovery and kindness and finding your way, even if it didn't look like anyone else's.

That clarity gave me the confidence to keep expanding.

I launched monthly crystal subscriptions for those who loved a surprise and a deeper connection to the seasons and moon cycles. I began writing my own full moon and new moon rituals, drawing on years of personal practice. I created bundles that encouraged journaling, intention setting and self-care. I introduced a members-only group where people could connect with each other, learn more about crystals and receive monthly rituals and prompts.

Slowly, it started to feel like I wasn't just building a brand – I was building a community.

People started to reach out not just as customers, but as humans. They told me how their children loved opening the parcels. How their affirmations were now stuck to their mirrors. How a certain crystal sat on their work desk to get them through the week. How they came back to the jars during grief, anxiety or burnout. That was the moment I realised this business wasn't small anymore. It wasn't about jars and parcels. It was about impact.

And alongside the products, something else was growing too – *me.*

I started showing up differently. With more trust in my voice. More belief in my vision. I took up space in rooms I used to shrink myself in. I said yes to podcast interviews and networking events. I talked about mindset, intention and values as much as I talked about crystals. I began stepping into my role not just as a seller, but as a guide. A mentor. A quiet voice reminding others what I had once needed to hear – *you are enough.*

The more I trusted myself, the more aligned everything became. I stopped second-guessing every decision. I stopped comparing my business to others. I started choosing ease over hustle. Intuition over industry trends. Community over competition.

One of the best decisions I made was to bring Tyler more into the heart of the brand. Not just in spirit, but visibly. People loved hearing that this was a legacy business. That it began with a child's idea and a mother's willingness to believe. That one day, it would belong to him.

That vision fuels me. I want him to inherit not just a profitable brand, but a purpose-led one. One that stands for empowerment, kindness and authenticity. One that shows him it's possible to build something beautiful without burning yourself out.

A Tinchy Bit of Sparkle will always be rooted in where it came from – a moment of possibility in the middle of a storm. But now, it's also a platform for prosperity. For helping others rise. For reminding people that they don't have to wait to be perfect before they take a step forward.

And if that isn't prosperity, I don't know what is.

Leaving a Legacy – A Business Built for Tyler

When I talk about A Tinchy Bit of Sparkle, I don't just talk about crystals or affirmations. I talk about legacy. About love. About creating something my son can one day step into with pride and purpose.

This business didn't begin as a legacy project, but it's become one.

Tyler has been part of it from the very start. Not just because the name came from one of his beautiful, innocent comments or because he helped spark the idea for our first affirmation jars, but because his energy is woven into every part of it. Every choice I make carries his influence. Every challenge I work through has him in mind. Every success feels sweeter because he's been part of the journey.

For me, legacy isn't about leaving behind a big brand or just a stream of income. It's about showing him what's possible. It's about planting the idea that you can build something that matters, even when the world says you're not ready or not enough. It's about teaching him that he's allowed to dream big and start small – that value isn't measured by likes or followers or how fast you grow, but by how aligned you stay with what you care about.

I want Tyler to see that his ideas matter. That his voice matters. That kindness and creativity can be the foundation of a successful life, not just an afterthought. I want him to know that even on the days where it felt like everything was falling apart, I kept choosing to show up. For myself. For our future. For the people we serve.

There are moments when I watch him help package orders or proudly tell someone about the business, and I get this sense of quiet pride. Not just in what we've created, but in who he's becoming because of it. He's learning without even realising it – watching how things work, listening to how I talk to customers, seeing what it means to build something from scratch and treat people with care.

He might not fully understand it yet, and I don't expect him to. Right now, he just knows this is something we do together. That it's special. That it belongs to both of us in different ways. That he had a hand in creating it. That's enough for now.

But one day, when he's older and looking for his own place in the world, I hope he remembers this. I hope he remembers the sparkle. The rituals. The way we turned pain into purpose and self-doubt into service. Whether he chooses to run the business or build his own path entirely, I want him to carry the lessons forward.

Because the truth is, the legacy isn't just in the products. It's in the way we think. The way we speak to ourselves. The way we lift others up. That's the inheritance I want to leave him. Something built with love. Something he can be proud of. Something that stands for compassion, courage and conscious growth.

And it goes beyond just our family.

Every time I get a message from someone who says one of our crystals helped them through a breakup, or one of our rituals helped them release years of grief, or a single affirmation helped them feel brave enough to start again, I'm reminded that this legacy reaches further than I ever imagined.

It's not about scale. It's about impact.

It's about those quiet, life-changing moments that happen in private. The woman crying on her bedroom floor who sees *"I am enough"* on her windowsill. The teenager who gets their first rose quartz from a parent. The friend who gifts a ritual jar instead of flowers during a hard time.

This is what I want Tyler to inherit. A business that *matters*. Not because it's flashy or fast-growing, but because it's rooted in truth. Because it's built on care. Because it shows that doing things your own way – with heart, with purpose, with intention – is more than enough.

And more than anything, I want him to see that I didn't wait until I felt ready. I didn't wait until life got easier. I chose to build in the middle of the mess. I chose to create light even while I was still healing. That's the kind of strength I hope he carries.

Because legacy isn't something we write in a will. It's something we live every day. In our values. In our choices. In the way we speak to ourselves and others. And in the way we decide, even in the smallest moments, to believe in possibility.

Possibility Is a Choice – And You Can Choose It, Too

If you've made it this far, I want you to pause and take a breath. Right now. Breathe in. Hold it. Let it go. That feeling? That's yours. That's presence. That's power.

Because no matter where you are in your journey, *possibility still exists for you*. It's not reserved for the "lucky ones" or the people with perfect plans or no self-doubt. It's for women like us. Women who are tired. Women who are scared. Women who have tried before and failed. Women who are holding things together while still craving something more.

I want you to know that you don't have to be ready. You don't have to have it all figured out. You don't have to be further along. You just have to *choose*. Choose to believe that a different version of your life is possible. Choose to take the first step, even if your hands are shaking.

For me, it started with one jar. One crystal. One affirmation. Not because I had a grand vision, but because I needed something to hold on to. Something that reminded me who I was underneath the exhaustion. Something that whispered, *"You're allowed to try again."*

So today, I want to offer you three small steps. Nothing overwhelming. Nothing complicated. Just gentle actions you can take to move closer to *your* version of prosperity.

1. Write one affirmation that reflects the version of you you're becoming.

Don't overthink it. Say it as if it's already true. Maybe it's *"I am worthy of rest"* or *"I trust myself to grow."* Stick it on your mirror. Repeat it every morning.

2. Choose one crystal that speaks to you.

Don't worry about what it's "supposed" to do. Just hold it. Notice how it makes you feel. Let it be a reminder that your energy matters and how you *feel* matters.

3. Ask yourself: *What's one thing I can do this week that future me will thank me for?*

It could be sending an email. Making a list. Resting. Saying no. Saying yes. Trust the answer. Act on it with love.

That's how it begins.

You don't need a perfect mindset. You don't need to be healed. You just need a little belief. A little sparkle. A little space to begin.

Possibility lives in the quiet moments. And you are worthy of every single one.

Closing Reflection – I Can and I Will

There are still days when that old voice shows up. The one that whispers, *"You're not doing enough."* The one that questions everything. That tells me I'm falling behind. That I'm not built for this.

But now, I know how to answer it.

I come back to the same words that held me when I had nothing else to hold. *I am enough. I can and I will.* That's not just a mantra anymore – it's a promise. To myself. To Tyler. To every woman reading this who's still standing in that place of self-doubt, wondering if she can really create the life she dreams of.

You can.

You don't have to be fearless to begin. You don't have to wait for permission. You are allowed to take up space. To build slowly. To start again. To do things your way.

The woman who once sat at her kitchen table surrounded by crystals and self-doubt is no longer hiding. She's leading. She's creating. She's teaching her son what it means to live with heart and intention.

Just the other week, I watched him hand a crystal to a customer at our stall, explaining what it was for with confidence in his voice. He beamed when they said thank you. I caught his eye, and in that moment, I realised – this isn't just legacy. This is *life*. This is love in motion.

And now I want the same for you.

You don't need to have all the answers. You just need to believe that they're worth looking for. You just need to know that your voice matters. That your ideas matter. That your healing, your magic, your version of prosperity – it all matters.

You're already enough, just as you are. But if you're ready to rise?

Say it with me:

"I can and I will."

Because you can, and you will.

Gillian Sneddon

Author

https://www.facebook.com/profile.php?id=61566570913038
https://www.instagram.com/GHSneddon

GH Sneddon was inspired to become a preschool author a few months after her son was born, when she discovered his love for books even as a tiny baby. His sunshine nature and her deep desire to show him the depths of her love, using the Louise L. Hay love principles she'd studied for over 20 years, led her to write a heartfelt book so he would always know he is loved, adored, and cherished. Gillian has always had a passion for helping children, supporting children's charities for three decades and buying Christmas gifts for children in care long before becoming a mother herself. Today, she volunteers at St Joseph's RC Primary School and with the children's charity Abernecessities, helping disadvantaged children in her community. Gillian also visits nurseries to read her book aloud—an experience that brings her great joy and allows her to share her message of love with many more little hearts.

A Little Ray of Sunshine

By Gillian Sneddon

I am so honored and excited to share the journey of how this book came to life—from a spark of possibility to a purpose that blossomed into something much bigger than myself. What began as a simple act of love for my baby boy has grown into a vision for children everywhere: that they may grow up surrounded by love, filled with confidence, and anchored in the knowledge that they are cherished exactly as they are.

The Spark of Love

It all began with my son. When he came into my life, he lit up my world like a little tornado of love, fun, and laughter. His energy was infectious; his laughter could light up the whole house. He was bright, enthusiastic, and full of curiosity. Every day, I felt at this profound responsibility—not just to care for him, but to nurture the kind of love that would shape who he would become.

I wanted him to always feel cherished, adored, and deeply loved. More than anything, I wanted him to know—without question—that he was light, he was sunshine, he was warmth. That his very presence was a gift, not just to me, but to the world.

As a new mother, I quickly realized that the early years with my child are more than just feeding, sleeping, and playing. They are about connection. They are about the first messages that get planted in a child's heart—messages that become the foundation of their self-worth. And I knew I wanted my son's first messages to be ones of unconditional love.

From Bedtime Books to a New Idea

Like most parents, I read to my son every day. We had a growing collection of sturdy board books, but his favorites were always the peekaboo flap books. He would giggle and squeal with delight every time a new picture was revealed. I cherished those moments of joy, those quiet snuggles at bedtime, those bursts of laughter in the middle of the afternoon.

But after a few months, a thought began to grow in my heart: *What if I could create a book just for him?* A book that wasn't only about animals or colors, but about who he was at his core. A book that would teach him not only numbers and days of the week, but also that he was loved and that he could love himself.

And so I began writing what would become **My Little Ray of Sunshine's Favorite Toys**. I kept it simple: seven sturdy pages with bright illustrations, playful repetition, and the things he loved most—his toys. But at the heart of it all were affirmations: **"I am loved. I love myself. I am a ray of sunshine."**

Last page was designed like a mirror of the heart, reflecting back the love I felt for him. I wanted him to see himself through loving eyes, to internalize that message before the world ever tried to tell him otherwise.

The Five Love Languages for Children

Later, something unexpected and beautiful unfolded. I realized that this little book naturally supported the five love languages Gary Chapman described in his bestselling work, ***The 5 Love Languages****.*

- **Words of Affirmation**.: Every page carried simple but powerful messages of love and self-worth.
- **Quality Time**.: Reading together created sacred moments of connection.

- **Acts of Service**.: Parents taking time to read was itself a loving service to the child.
- **Physical Touch**.: Cuddling together while reading made love tangible.
- **Gifts**.: The book itself became a token of love, a keepsake that could be treasured for years.

I remembered hearing a woman in a Tony Robbins class share how practicing the five love languages daily transformed the love within her family, she said it exploded love with her family members if she practiced the five love languages daily. In that moment, I had an epiphany: This is what my book could do for children everywhere - explode love. It could make love a daily habit, if my book was used as a daily tool to grow love. It could make affirmation, touch, and connection part of bedtime, morning routines, or quiet afternoons, exploding love in family units.

For the Children Who Need It Most

While the book was written for every child, my heart especially went out to those who needed it most: disadvantaged children, sick children, and little ones who might not feel that daily warmth of love.

I began posting images of the book going out to children's charities on my social media. Soon, I found myself volunteering at a wonderful Scottish charity called *Abernecessities*. They cared deeply for families, providing, best of the best preloved clothes, food packs, toiletries, preloved cribs, buggies, toys and even catered for children's birthdays with a beautiful bakers cake and birthday decorations — helping moms and children feel seen, supported, and special.

When I offered to donate 20 books, they embraced the idea instantly. Within 24 hours, copies were being placed into baby cribs delivered to disadvantaged families. That moment brought me to tears. For so long, I had dreamed of my book reaching children who would need the daily message of love the most—and here it was, happening before my eyes.

Even more touching was learning that many families supported were single mothers and survivors of domestic violence, beginning fresh. Knowing that my book could bring even a small measure of comfort, reassurance, and joy to those children filled my heart with purpose.

Inspired by Louise Hay

Another source of inspiration for this journey was Louise L. Hay. I began my own self-love practice at the age of 30 when I was gifted **You Can Heal Your Life** *by a lovely local woman named Aileen, a Louise Hay-trained teacher.*

Over the next seven years, I learned from her and from Hay House authors, especially Dr. David Hamilton, a kind Scottish author whose warmth and sincerity left a lasting impression on me. He showed me that success and kindness could walk hand in hand. When he released his book, **I Heart Me**, I was deeply honored to be thanked within its pages for a small role I had played in his journey.

These lessons shaped my vision for my own book. I wanted to weave Louise Hay's affirmations into its pages so children could build strong self-worth from the earliest age. Whether it was saying "**I love you**" in the mirror or hearing **"You're my little ray of sunshine,"** the goal was to plant seeds of self-love and confidence that would grow throughout their lives.

Why This Book Matters

At this point, you might be wondering: What makes this little book so important? Why does it matter that children hear these affirmations so early?

Research in child development shows that the earliest years of life are when self-image begins to take root. The words children hear, the tone of voice used, the expressions of love they receive—all of these create the first building blocks of how they see themselves. When children grow up hearing **"You are loved,"** they begin to believe it. When they repeat **"I love myself,"** they start to internalize self-respect and self-worth.

This book isn't just a bedtime story. It's a tool. It's a gentle, joyful way to give children the language of love and self-worth before the world tries to convince them otherwise.

The Ripple Effect

Imagine a child who grows up reading **My Little Ray of Sunshine's Favorite Toys** *every night. Imagine them entering school already knowing they are loved, already confident in their identity as someone who matters. Imagine the resilience they carry when challenges come, the kindness they extend to others, the light they bring into classrooms, friendships, and eventually workplaces and families of their own.*

Now imagine hundreds, even thousands of children with that same foundation. That is the ripple effect I dream of. This little book, read in living rooms, bedrooms, and nursery classrooms around the world, can help create a generation of children who know their worth and extend love outwardly.

Stories That Could Be

Picture this:

- *A child in a hospital bed, clutching the book as a comfort item during treatment.*
- *A father working long hours, coming home to read it as his bedtime ritual, bonding with his child in those few sacred minutes.*

- *A teacher using it in a nursery classroom, helping children learn not only numbers and days of the week, but also kindness and love affirmations.*
- *A foster parent gifting it to a child on their first night in a new home, reassuring them they are loved.*

These aren't just possibilities. —They are visions of what is already beginning to happen as the book reaches more children.

The Benefits in Full

To summarize the benefits, **My Little Ray of Sunshine's Favorite Toys** *offers:*

- **Affirmations of Self-Worth**.: Planting seeds of love, belonging, and confidence.
- **Bonding Moments**.: Creating daily opportunities for parent-child connection after growing love.
- **Educational Learning**.: Teaching numbers, days of the week, colours, toys and fun noises, and memory skills.
- **Support for Love Language**s.: Making love visible, audible, and tangible every day.
- **Charitable Impact**.: Providing comfort and joy to disadvantaged and vulnerable children.
- **Generational Legacy**.: Helping raise children who grow into adults capable of loving themselves and others deeply.

A Humble Invitation

And so, **My Little Ray of Sunshine's Favorite Toys** *is more than just a children's book. It's a vessel for love. It's a gentle companion for bedtime, a tool for learning, and a seed planter for lifelong self-worth.*

When you place this book in the hands of a child, you are not just giving them pages. —You are giving them affirmation, joy, and the building blocks of a confident, kind and loving life. When you choose to gift this book to many children—to nieces, nephews, nursery classrooms, hospitals, or charities—you multiply that ripple of love.

My dream is simple: That every child, everywhere, has at least one book that tells them they are loved, they are sunshine, and they are worthy.

So I humbly extend this invitation humbly, from my heart: Help me spread the love and sunshine. Whether to one child or to many, let this little book be a reminder that love, once planted, grows far beyond the pages.

Thank You

I am deeply grateful to Anisa and Natosha for welcoming me to share my story and book through their book and docuseries. Being part of Possibility to Prosperity is truly a wonderful honor and privilege, and I feel so blessed to have this opportunity and it's been nothing short of exhilarating. These two incredible women inspire me with their kindness, dedication, and tireless work. They have guided and supported me so thoughtfully along the way, and the journey with them has been both uplifting and empowering. From my heart, thank you, Anisa and Natosha. May God bless you both abundantly.

You can buy a copy of my Little Ray Of Sunshine's Favourite Toys from the link below.

https://www.tiktok.com/@mylittleray?_t=ZN-90A2qWgHNm2&_r=1

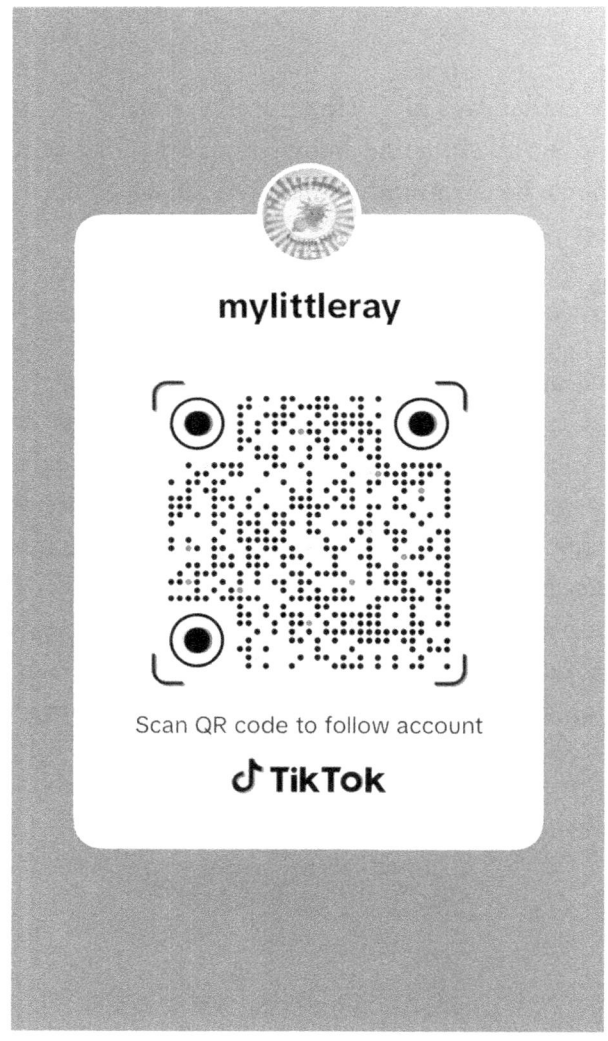

✧ Join the Million Dollar Mom Society Movement. ✧

Step into our world of possibility and prosperity.

Visit our website <u>HERE</u> to be part of it.

<u>https://www.milliondollarmom.org/</u>

www.ingramcontent.com/pod-product-compliance
Lightning Source LLC
Chambersburg PA
CBHW071724120626
46550CB00002B/376